About the Author:

A career in the highly-rewarded world of the financial services was calling. After a successful career in the Royal Navy, Martin May-Clingo was paying his own way through the rigorous training to become an Independent Financial Advisor when the Global Financial Crisis (GFC) of 2007/08 hit and economies around the world collapsed. Millions lost their livelihoods and, in its wake, the GFC swept away all opportunities for Martin to enter the industry. So, a change of direction ensued which saw him open his own businesses in internet marketing and social media. It was during this period, that in 2013, Martin chanced upon Bitcoin. The possibilities of the future of cryptocurrency immediately captivated him and he has been sharing its journey ever since. It's not been without its lows and he has learnt some hard and costly lessons; however, it has most certainly had its highs!

In this book, "Understanding Bitcoin & Cryptocurrency … Beginners Guide to the Crypto Revolution" Martin lays out, in the clearest way, what Bitcoin is, how the system works and how to get your own Bitcoin, as well as the risks and the opportunities to enable you to make an informed decision on your entry into this exciting new world order. He also provides an introduction into the wider cryptocurrency world and has compiled a guide to the current Top Five Cryptocurrencies by global valuation.

Warning

Cryptocurrencies, including Bitcoin, are high risk and if considered for investment purposes currently highly speculative. Therefore, they may not be suitable for everyone. They are considered high risk and you can lose some, or all, of your money, so never risk more than you can afford to lose.

In the UK the Financial Conduct Authority does not regulate the cryptocurrency market, nor do any regulatory authorities in any other country of the world at the time of writing. This means that in the UK you would not have the protection of the Financial Ombudsman Service or The Financial Services Compensation Scheme; similarly, this is likely to be the situation in most other countries of the world. Seek independent financial advice if you are unsure of the suitability of any investment or purchase of Cryptocurrencies, including Bitcoin.

This book does not recommend any particular cryptocurrency, including Bitcoin, crypto exchange or crypto wallet. The information provided in good faith in this book is simply to educate the reader and does not constitute investment advice or advice of any kind.

Be informed. Be safe.

Copyright

Understanding Bitcoin & Cryptocurrency
Beginners Guide to the Crypto Revolution
Copyright 2018 Martin May-Clingo

This publication is designed to provide accurate and
authoritative information in regard to the subject matter
covered. It is sold with the understanding that the
publisher is not engaged in rendering legal, accounting or
other professional services. If you require legal advice or
other expert assistance, you should seek the services of a
competent professional.

Understanding Bitcoin

& Cryptocurrency

...Beginners Guide to the Crypto Revolution

*<u>Plus - Bonus Guide to the **Top Five** Cryptocurrencies!</u>*

Contents

Section 2

Chapter 1

Bitcoin - The Genesis

As is my habit on a long flight I gather up in an armful of reading material from the airport bookstores prior to embarking. Even on the longest flights I can only tolerate a maximum of two movies, although ideally one satisfies my viewing needs and so for the rest of the flight, in between bouts of restless sleep, I need to read. It was during one such long haul flight to Southeast Asia in December 2013 that I stumbled across an interesting article about something called 'Bitcoin' and 'Cryptocurrency'.

It really grabbed my attention. It seemed so futuristic and yet compelling. So, over the next three weeks during my stay in Southeast Asia I spent a lot of my free time researching on the Internet everything that I could find about Bitcoin and the brave new world of Cryptocurrencies.

Whilst Bitcoin had been around for 4 years, Cryptocurrencies generally were very much in an embryonic period. Even so Bitcoin mining (of which more later) was already relatively advanced and required significant computing power and so I researched alternatives which were more within the reach of my modest means. On my return to the UK I immediately made my first purchase of Bitcoin and corralled the family's computers for the mining of a crypto known as Quark!

So began my crypto journey which has by no means been a straight and easy road. Nevertheless, I have learnt invaluable lessons which I am now able to put to good use in my own cryptocurrency dealings and, more importantly, to share with you so that you can avoid the same mistakes and benefit from my experience to accelerate your entry into the exciting new world of cryptocurrency, should you choose to do so. I've been researching, analysing and invested in Bitcoin since 2013; I've seen it increase in value by thousands of percent to become one of the most Googled subjects across the world.

Conceptually Bitcoin was born in a White Paper written in 2008 by the famously mysterious character, Satoshi Nakomoto.

For the average person in the street the technology behind Bitcoin is incredibly complicated whilst the concept and the day-to-day usage of it is very straightforward. This is not really a problem for most if you just stop for a moment to consider what is it that you need to understand. Take for example flying, most people have no knowledge whatsoever of the complex mechanical, electrical and digital technology within the aircraft on which they're flying. In fact, a large number of people don't have any idea of the basic aerodynamics! What every passenger flying understands is how to book the flight, the embarkation process and the on-board video on demand control - and that's about it! The necessary level of knowledge & understanding for most people to use Bitcoin is similar.

It seems that the Global Financial Crisis (GFC) of 2007/08 was the catalyst for the launch of Bitcoin. However, the seed of the idea was planted many years before as can be seen in the references to the GFC in the 2008 White Paper by Satoshi Nakamoto.

Although there has been continuous low-level media coverage about Bitcoin and Cryptocurrencies since its launch, it is only since the beginning of 2017 that there has been wide scale media and public interest across the world. We have been regaled with stories of individuals investing a few hundred dollars at the beginning of the decade who have now become millionaires; tales of woe of Bitcoin millions lost after laptops were accidentally discarded; Pyramid investing and worse scams. Forecasts of Bitcoin climbing to valuations of $250,000; forecasts of Bitcoin crashing to zero!

Of course these media stories always seek to sensationalise. After all, that's how they sell newspapers and get you to watch their news station. By now, in this era of *'fake news'*, we should all know to be wary of the headlines. Such stories can create a sense of panic and bewilderment, a fear of missing out (FOMO), or a sense that it's all simply too risky.

What I seek to do in this book, is to strip away the sensationalist headlines and lay out the facts to help you understand the risks and the opportunities that Bitcoin and Cryptocurrencies present. I'm not going to try to persuade you to invest in Bitcoin or any other Cryptocurrencies; merely present the facts to enable you to decide if you wish to hold Bitcoin, show you how to do so relatively safely.

Be in no doubt though, Bitcoin and its underlying technology is the start of a radical shift in power from which you will benefit, whether you decide to become actively involved or not.

This is the beginning of the *Crypto Revolution.*

Chapter 2

Why Do We Even Need Bitcoin?

Of course, life as we know it would continue to be sustained without Bitcoin. Much in the same way that the world would continue spinning if we did not have the Internet. The point being that technological developments evolve and improve the lives of people if not the world itself; and Bitcoin and its underlying Blockchain technology have the potential to exponentially improve the lives of all citizens of the world in so many different ways.

But first we need to step back to the time proceeding Bitcoin. The financial system of the world has itself evolved over thousands of years from the time of barter through to the introduction of coinage with precious metal content, (primarily gold & silver), paper currencies backed by Kingdoms and nation states up to the 21st-century use of electronic currencies backed by central banks enabling the use of pieces of plastic, (credit & debit cards), to purchase goods. A common requirement that accompanied this evolution has been *'trust'* between the parties involved; the payer and the payee.

Whilst on the whole trust has been maintained, there are (at least) tens of millions of cases where this trust has been broken. Daily fraudulent use of credit cards occurs across the world, resulting in increased costs of goods for everyone as well as many personal tales of woe from the individuals and small businesses who have been defrauded. A major flaw in the current system of our currencies backed by central banks, is that central banks are more often than not controlled or influenced behind the scenes by their political master's in government. The decisions taken by those in power are not always in the best interests of people that they are supposed to serve. So often those decisions may be made to ensure retention of political power and/or for personal benefits; often illicitly amassing and retaining huge amounts of wealth.

When we speak of people in power, it is not just those in political office, but also powerful unelected business people - CEO's. There are now many companies whose capitalisation (value) is greater than the GDP of many countries. For example, Apple, Amazon, Google, AliBaba, HSBC, Exon Mobile, JP Morgan Chase, Tencent, etc, etc.

The decisions made by the CEOs & Boards of many large companies have a direct and significant impact on the lives of many people. And I don't just mean their employees or their customers or their shareholders. Think back to the GFC of 2007/08; this was a direct result of disastrous decisions by banks and large financial institutions, which were primarily driven by greed. And whilst these greedy financiers were harvesting their illicit gains before the storm of the GFC, our political leaders who should have been holding them to account were at best sleeping on the job or at worst turning a blind eye whilst they sipped champagne as guests in corporate boxes. The direct consequences of their greed was a global economic downturn in which millions of people across the world lost their livelihoods and in many cases their homes too.

Around the world, as I write this, millions of ordinary people are struggling to support their families in circumstances where their nation's economy has been devastated by their own political leaders. Think oil-rich Venezuela, bountiful Argentina, or in Europe the nation of timeless myths, Greece.

How many of you remember the aftermath of the GFC in your own country? Every country in the world was affected and the taxpayer had to bail out the banks, which had caused the crisis in the first place, from going bankrupt. Taxpayers were not asked if they agreed to bail out the banks; governments took the decision to use our money whether you liked it or not. Many people were fearful that they were going to lose their life savings and queued around the block to withdraw their deposits from the banks. Were you one of them?

Against this backdrop, Satoshi Nakamoto took the decision that the world was ready for a radical new approach to currency. An approach that would re-establish trust in a currency itself, an approach that would restore and ensure trust between parties in a transaction, an approach that will level the playing field for ordinary men and women across the world. And so, entered the world Bitcoin; effectively firing the starting gun for a new wave of technology with the potential to dramatically improve the lives of all people in so many ways. That technology is called Blockchain.

So now in the second decade of the 21st-century with rising global awareness and communications interconnectivity, the masses of people are understanding how their trust has been betrayed. Did you know that since 2009 global economic growth has reached record levels – and have you felt the benefits? Whilst political leaders enjoy their gold-plated benefits and CEOs raise their own salaries and bonuses to astronomical levels to ensure they retain their position as a member of the '*1%*', (*1% of the global population own 82% of the wealth*), the masses of workers across the world have seen their standard of living stagnate or even decline.

And yet, despite this phenomenal economic growth, governments continue to mismanage their economies and appear not to have learnt lessons from the GFC. Debt has risen to historic record levels in 2018; in the UK government debt is over 120% of GDP compared to 63% in 2007. In the USA we frequently hear of the government having to temporarily shut down services as their debt level reaches the Congress legislated Federal Debt Ceiling. What you need to understand from this, is that another GFC may not be too far away!

In its 2017 Global Risks Report, The World Economic Forum identified *"profound social instability"* as the biggest global risk for the next 10 years. This risk was assessed on a range of factors.

What is relevant to this book is the major consequent damage such instability could have on national fiat currencies. Just consider recent history and you will see the deep traumatic shock that currencies experienced because of the social instability usually as a result of conflict but not always; for example, the former Yugoslavia, Iraq, Syria, Zimbabwe, Venezuela. Not so extreme, but other countries have seen their currencies significantly devalued as a result of internal turmoil including Turkey, Mexico, South Africa, and even the UK post the BREXIT vote, (UK voting to leave the European Union). Consequently, I believe that Cryptocurrencies such as Bitcoin will become the safe haven for huge numbers of people across the world.

So how does Bitcoin improve our lives?

Well you need to understand where we are now. Wherever you are when it comes to financial transactions there is an added price to pay; and it's a high price. Unless you are paying in cash, which is increasingly more and more difficult to do, (another government hidden agenda, but that's not for this book!), there are always financial intermediaries – middlemen - involved. Generally, they are banks, credit card companies, lawyers, cross-border currency exchanges. And all these financial intermediaries take a cut, a fee or a commission, from your transaction pushing up the cost to you.

For most people, buying their home is generally the most expensive purchase they will make in a lifetime. If you are buying a house and you're ready to complete the contract, you usually must send the money due to your lawyer who then sends it to the bank of the seller's lawyer who then sends it to the bank account of the seller. At each point that the money moves someone would be charging a fee for simply moving the money onwards. Now this may seem quite reasonable if it was a small amount. But it's not a small amount. Typically, in the UK today, to transfer any sum over £10,000 same day the bank will charge you £35 (about $50). Now these charges are levied at each point of transfer so it's possible that the same bank would be making £105 ($150) moving the money, account to account, in their bank. What makes these charges even harder to swallow is that the payer is likely to be doing the actual work in arranging the transfer and the banks computerised automated systems then action the transfer order!

Millions of people the world over including myself, regularly transfer money abroad. I'm not just talking about businesses, but about millions of expats working abroad and sending money home to their families – referred to as Remittances. These people are a rich source of easy money for the financial institutions. In 2017 a total of $444 billion was remitted across the world. In the UK remittances charges of 5-7% are common, not forgetting also that the remittance companies take their additional hidden fees from the spread in the exchange rates.   Furthermore, it's not an instant transfer. I personally have had to wait for up to 7 days to receive my money in my account abroad. Where has it been? It's been sitting in the bank's account earning them, not me, interest. Also, as well as the financial institution in the country you are sending from charging you, the bank at the receiving end may also impose additional charges.

You would think that it could not get worse than that. But it does.

In Western Europe we actually have relatively low charges compared to many other parts of the world. In some countries in south-east Asia the banks will charge you to send money to another account at another branch of the same bank. Unbelievable! I experienced this in the Philippines where they will charge you 100 pesos (about £1.40) to send the equivalent of £10. I still recall the bank clerk saying to me, "...and of course there is our charge." and I responded, rather irritated "there is nothing *of course*, ...it's your bank's decision!"

Whenever you decide to pay by credit card; the financial intermediaries are literally laughing all the way to the bank. Why do you think Warren Buffet, probably the world's most successful investor, invests in MasterCard? Of course, if you pay off your balance by the due date you are not charged anything, but woe betide you if you don't meet your commitment as the banks will surely take their pound of flesh in the form of interest charged at typically between 15-20%, but can be as high as 40% - at a time when Base Rates are just 0.5%!

But small businesses also suffer at the hands of the financial intermediaries. Every time you use your piece of plastic, the credit or debit card, the business has to pay a fee or commission. I have a small business in the UK which accepts credit and debit cards; my service provider was Barclaycard Merchant Services. When I started with them in 2000 they were charging me a commission of 4.95% and held on to my money for 30 days as they said my business was high risk from default.

After a few years I did manage to negotiate down to 3.95% but they still retained a 30-day holding period. In 2013, 13 years after I first signed up, I asked them to give me a better deal and they refused. So, I signed up with a competitor and now pay 1.95% and get my money within three days!

Can you believe it? Barclaycard Merchant Services called me in 2015 and asked to go back to them as they could offer me a better deal! I said 'no way' after they treated me so badly and effectively ripped me off for 13 years. Maybe I should have been a better businessman and negotiated harder; however, the point I want to illustrate here is how financial intermediaries always win, no matter what.

So to summarise, the financial system which we have endured for over a century has ripped you off, lacked adequate security to prevent large-scale fraud and has betrayed your trust. Bitcoin is fast, secure and low-cost in comparison.

Bitcoin seeks to level the playing field in favour of the ordinary man and woman.

Chapter 3

What Is Bitcoin and How Does It Work?

To some it is almost an existential question. What is Bitcoin? Despite the fact that people are trading Bitcoin the world over, a number of influential people question whether Bitcoin is even a 'thing'. However, the debate has primarily been on *defining* whether Bitcoin is-

- a currency
- a security
- an asset
- a store of value
- a combination of the above
- none of the above

Such debate may seem somewhat irrelevant to day-to-day users of Bitcoin. Nevertheless, to government authorities defining Bitcoin it is considered vital. If it's an asset or a security, then it can be taxed; if it's simply a security then it would be necessary to subject it to a raft of regulations that are generally applicable to the trading of stocks &

shares. If it is defined as a combination of those, it will make it particularly tricky to regulate and then administer the regulations. At the time of writing debate continues.

When discussions around Bitcoin being a *store of value* occur, the usual comparison is to gold. For thousands of years gold has been considered the ultimate store of value by people across the world. In times of crisis, people have converted cash and other assets into gold. Of course, the price of gold can fluctuate quite substantially dependent upon demand; which increases dramatically in times of crisis. There may be some merit to considering Bitcoin as a *store of value* as already in its short life it has been what people have turned to during acute economic crisis in their countries. Zimbabwe and Venezuela being two recent examples where, due to government incompetence and corruption, inflation became rampant and out of control resulting in food, fuel and medicine shortages thus creating immense hardship for the people whose pay simply couldn't keep up with the rising prices.

Other similarities between Bitcoin and gold is that both our 'mined'. Gold is mined in the traditional sense from the ground whereas Bitcoin is mined digitally; (I'll explain this in more detail shortly). Also, both have a finite supply which enhances their reputations as a store of value.

As well as being a store of value Bitcoin and gold have further utility, although this is where the similarities diverge. Gold is used extensively in jewellery and is considered the number one precious metal for this. More and more gold is used in high technology equipment, particularly computers and smartphones. Bitcoin's utility is as a currency, a cryptocurrency.

As the debate about the definition of Bitcoin rumbles on, I cannot help but wonder if the great and good heading governments and government agencies have actually read the short White Paper written by Satoshi Nakamoto. For if they have they would have seen that Satoshi Nakamoto answers the question in the very first line of the White Paper indeed it is in the title the White Paper:

"Bitcoin: A Peer-to-Peer Electronic Cash System"

What can be clearer than that? He clearly designed and developed Bitcoin to become a global currency unconstrained by geographic borders, not dependent on any government or central bank.

He designed Bitcoin to be:

- Decentralised
- Trustless
- Anonymous

I will explain these principle elements of Bitcoin in detail shortly.

The most obvious difference between the fiat currencies you are familiar with - dollars, pounds, euros, etc and Bitcoin is that you can physically hold the former. Fiat currencies are those currencies guaranteed by a government; state issued money. Sometimes this lack of apparent tangibility of Bitcoin causes some unease amongst people. If you can't hold it, touch it; how can it be real? But think of the number of times you have purchased something on a credit or debit card; the seller quite happily accepted this form of payment without seeing your cash. Also have you ever transferred money from account to account? Again, you would not physically carry the cash and hand it over to the other account holder. So, think of Bitcoin in similar terms; as a digital currency (essentially computer code) that operates like an 'App'; it's not tangible but it is real!

How It Works in Practice

Bitcoin is mined. It is digitally mined; not mined in the traditional sense of digging coal or gold out of the ground. Nevertheless, the effort required to mine Bitcoin in terms of computer power is substantial. For a miner to be rewarded with Bitcoin he is required to provide the solution to a complex problem known as an algorithm. However, algorithm problem-solving is competitive with other miners; so all miners using their computer power are attempting to solve the problem first and so be rewarded with Bitcoin. As soon as an algorithm is solved, effectively all miners restart in attempting to solve a new algorithm, which is always progressively harder than the previous one.

When the 1st Bitcoin were mined in 2009 by Satoshi Nakamoto the reward, for solving the algorithm and therefore mining a *'block'* was 50 Bitcoin. To ensure a progressive release of Bitcoin, the reward is halved when a pre-defined milestone in number of blocks mined is completed. At the time of writing, the block reward is currently 12.5 coins. So, the reward is reducing quite substantially.

Miners remain motivated to mine despite this due to the huge increase in the value of Bitcoin but also as they are rewarded for effectively running the *network*. Each miner is known as a 'node' and when Bitcoin transactions take place it is the nodes that validate them. In return for their service in validating transactions, nodes are rewarded; a very small percentage of the transaction value. Therefore, even when all Bitcoins are mined, forecast to be around 2040, miners will continue to have an important ongoing role in maintaining the Bitcoin network.

Whilst you might understandably be interested in mining Bitcoin yourself, I must tell you that unless you are already incredibly wealthy and willing to invest a lot of money in mining rigs, (computers dedicated to mining), the opportunity has passed you by. In fact, when I investigated Bitcoin back in 2013, it was already a consensus that it was too late for me to get into mining. The reason is that some, now very rich, miners have effectively cornered the market and to mine profitably requires banks of ASIC (Application-Specific Integrated Circuit) computers which are expensive and require a lot of electricity to run. Consequently, the main players now have literally warehouses full of ASIC miners often located in very cold regions to reduce the cost of air conditioning as these ASIC computers produce an astounding amount of heat. Therefore, as this is a

Beginners Guide, I'm not going to go into any further detail on mining.

I've got a little ahead of myself here. Back to the mined Bitcoin and the resolved 'block'; what happens next?

Bitcoin effectively has its own secure accounting system which ensures the prevention of fraud within the system; unlike fiat currency (dollars, pounds, euros etc) which can be counterfeited, it is impossible to counterfeit a Bitcoin. It does this by using a technology known as *'Blockchain'*.

The Blockchain enables the storage, validation, authorisation and movement of data and digital transactions across the internet. It is a continuous link of blocks which cannot be broken once validated; within the blocks will be the details of transactions related to a particular Bitcoin; from its first being mined and its onward history of validated transactions infinitum.

The accounting system run on the Blockchain is known as a *'distributed ledger'* and is integral to it. Ledgers have been kept in the systems of accounting since the days of the ancient Egyptian Pharaoh's if not before. They have evolved from carvings in stone, writings on papyrus then paper and lately accounting software packages. So ledgers are nothing new. What is new is that the ledger is *distributed,* and it is this which helps to give Bitcoin its power through its decentralised nature enabling a secure *'trustless'* system.

Rather than keeping records of all the Bitcoin transactions on a central database with its inherent vulnerability to hacking or denial of service attacks, the Bitcoin transactions are spread around randomly on nodes across the globe. It is not reliant on any one computer, database or nation states to keep it running - this is what is meant by *'trustless'*. <u>You can trust it</u> because you don't have to trust any one entity, as the decentralised distributed ledger provides you unparalleled security.

Traditional centralised database

Distributed Ledger on nodes across the world.

The intermediaries, such as banks, currency exchanges etc are no longer needed. So, there is no need to pay their fees, (which are often hidden in the margin), so saving you money at the same time as enjoying improved security.

The third essential component that makes Bitcoin unique is the anonymity/privacy that it provides. To understand that I will now explain the process of transacting using Bitcoin.

In a later chapter I will take you through the process of acquiring and securing your Bitcoin. For the moment we will assume that you already own Bitcoin, which means you have already set up the security protocols for your Bitcoin wallets and have a *'private key'* and a *'public key'*. The terms are self-explanatory but for the avoidance of doubt a private key is essentially a form of encrypted access which is private to you and should be shared with no one else. A public key is rather like an account number (but much longer) and you will share with others who wish to send you Bitcoin. This is my public key and you are more than welcome to send a test transfer donation to this address:

3NYms3TTVDsEQYwuj1fgQxwnyQNSQ5spFF

Say you wish to send Mrs Jones 0.5 Bitcoin, this is an example process:
- Mrs Jones advises you of her public key
- You open your encrypted Bitcoin wallet with your private key
- You enter the send Bitcoin area of your wallet and then enter Mrs Jones public key and the amount of Bitcoin you wish to send; in this case 0.5 Bitcoin.
- You hit the submit button and the transaction is now loaded onto the Blockchain.
- Using the decentralised distributed ledger with decentralised nodes your transaction is

validated by a minimum six nodes to ensure this is a valid transaction (i.e. to prevent the same Bitcoin being spent twice)

- As soon as the minimum number of nodes have validated the transaction, it is confirmed on the Blockchain and Mrs Jones will see the 0.5 Bitcoin in her own encrypted Bitcoin wallet.
- The transaction is now complete.

SEND BITCOINS

⚠ Make sure you have the correct beneficiary address. **More Information**

AMOUNT	25 BTC MAX
	USD 165,450.25
RECIPIENT BITCOIN ADDRESS	3NYms3TTVDsEQYwuj1fgQxwnyQNSQ5spFF
ACCOUNT TO DEBIT	My account (BTC 0) ⌄ ●
TRANSACTION FEES	Standard (normal confirmation) ⌄
TOTAL SPENT	BTC 25.000008 (incl. BTC 0.000008 of transaction fees)
	USD 165,450.30 (incl. USD 0.05 of transaction fees)

CANCEL   SEND

Sending Bitcoin is simple!

Now when Mrs Jones sees the 0.5 Bitcoin in her wallet it will show her the public key address that it was sent from, but she will not necessarily know who the owner of the account is. Now the actual transaction is public on the Blockchain, <u>it is not hidden</u>. However, the parties involved in the transaction are anonymous.

The transaction now on the Blockchain is immutable; cannot be deleted, redacted, amended. The proof will be there for all time that the payment of 0.5 Bitcoin was made by you and was received by Mrs Jones - although your and Mrs Jones's personal details will be anonymized. The immutability of transactions on the Blockchain is an incredibly powerful factor in cryptocurrency as I will explore in a later chapter.

So, I hope you can now understand how the highly complex Bitcoin is in fact very simple to use for day-to-day transactions.

Chapter 4

FAD or Scam or Both?

FAD (definition): - *an intense and widely shared enthusiasm for something, especially one that is short-lived and without basis in the object's qualities*

Bitcoin has been around for nearly a decade; it has increased in value and has clear real-world long-term utility. It is not a fad!

Look at history. In the early 20th century people thought the motor car a fad until Henry Ford demonstrated otherwise. In the late 1980s, mobile phones were considered a fad available only to rich city types, and yet now there are an estimated 5 billion mobile phones in the world; even children have them. Texting was initially considered a fad; now about 20 billion texts are sent every day. The Internet was even called a fad in the 1990s - I'll say no more on that!

Of the 195 countries in the world only five have totally banned Bitcoin; small countries with weak economies fearful of the downside effect on their own national currencies. One of them, showing incredible state hypocrisy, Venezuela, has launched its own state backed petrol cryptocurrency. Conversely many countries are scrambling to become cryptocurrency centres of excellence; Switzerland, Japan, Malta, Eire and Slovenia to name just a few. Recognising this trend, the City of London has belatedly realised that it's behind the curve and is now working feverishly to establish the city as a European centre for cryptocurrency.

Personally, I'm convinced that history will show that Bitcoin is not a fad, but in fact the springboard for the new cryptocurrency and Blockchain age.

But a Scam?

It is generally accepted concept in psychology that the two main drivers of humans are 'fear' and 'greed'. Now you may not agree with this; you may believe, as I do, that many people are driven by the desire to help their fellow man; do we not see this in the mother's care for her child, or the devotion and selflessness of many charity workers, some who put their lives at risk to help others in need. Nevertheless, for the purposes of this discussion, those drivers of fear and greed are highly relevant.

FOMO is an acronym I mentioned earlier in this book - Fear of Missing Out. This is very prevalent in the current somewhat febrile cryptocurrency climate. This fear is predicated on the belief that the opportunity to make money from cryptocurrency is slipping away. And this is partly a widespread hysteria fermented by the media and then pumped-up by an individual's natural greed. Do not allow FOMO to take over; take time to study and understand the facts before you make your decision on whether to get involved in cryptocurrency. If you do this you will see that there are many, many opportunities now and likely to be in the future.

Fear is also an emotion that can lead to a state of 'action paralysis'. With so many sensational headlines relating to Bitcoin and Cryptocurrencies swirling through the media many people are confused and have a sense of fear. Some government agencies seem laser focused and very vocal on the risks of money laundering, organised crime and financing of terrorism. Also, we hear of scams, pyramid-selling/Ponzi schemes, hacking and outright theft. The fear created by the heightened perspective on these issues can prevent some people from 'seeing the wood for the trees'. In other words, they cannot see through the headlines to the opportunity and so remain in the state of 'action paralysis'.

So, let's look at these issues. For, of course they are very real issues which need to be addressed. We will look at them issue by issue to put them in perspective.

Money laundering is a problem that governments have been dealing with for decades - well before the arrival of Cryptocurrencies. Internationally there is now much better concerted action to counter money-laundering. In many countries now if you deposit or transfer more than a certain amount of money you would have to prove its legal origin. In the UK I think that figure is currently any amount over £9000, but quite often banks will question you about the origin of lesser sums. However, this ensures that the law-abiding citizen is accountable, but criminals don't care about this and still find ways to launder their illicit gains, which are often huge sums of money. So, yes cryptocurrency could be used to money-launder; but law enforcement agencies have ways and the technology to follow the money, even if it's cryptocurrency. Let's be clear, the purpose of Cryptocurrencies is not to enable illegal activities and money-laundering; but like all things that are produced for the good of mankind those with evil intent will seek to corrupt and pervert for their own ends.

Here are just some of the major banks that have been alleged to have been used for money-laundering with regular nation-state currencies in the past few years:

Commonwealth Bank of Australia
HSBC
Industrial and Commercial Bank of China
Royal Bank of Scotland
Danske Bank
Deutsche Bank
An unnamed Canadian bank!
Citibank

I unearthed this information after a quick search on the Internet! You can do the same and you will find many, many more banks that, despite the money-laundering laws, are still being used in this way. So clearly concerns about money-laundering using Cryptocurrencies, whilst legitimate, are very much a small part of the larger international picture. The fact that dollars and pounds and all other currencies are being laundered by criminals does not stop those currencies being used legitimately every minute of every day across the world; so why should such a concern prevent you from using Cryptocurrencies.

A similar scenario emerges with respect to concerns about organised crime. There have been many headlines about Cryptocurrencies being used for the purchase of drugs and weapons. This has happened. However, these illegal trades constituted an incredibly small percentage of the overall transactions, which were conducted using regular nation-state currencies. Law enforcement agencies actively investigating organised crime do not make a distinction dependent on the currencies used in drugs and arms dealing. A few years ago, there was a lot of interest in what is known as the 'Dark Web', effectively a shadow Internet in which the technology makes it virtually impossible to trace those persons using it; whether for legitimate or illegal purposes. For we should not assume that those using the Dark Web are always criminals; there are a significant number of citizens who simply do not wish government agencies to be able to monitor their activities, and this is their right. However, law-enforcement agencies are tenacious, take the long view and have access to cutting-edge technology; and so, the Dark Web has not prevented them from bringing to justice criminals using it.

Perhaps the most notorious case that we know of is that of the Silk Road website that operated on the Dark Web and facilitated drug dealing, which has been indisputably linked to the deaths of at least six people. The criminal mastermind behind it, Mr Ross Ulbricht, was sentenced to life in prison in the USA in 2015 after an operation by the FBI brought down his criminal empire. Additionally, the court ordered Ulbricht to forfeit $184,000,000!

Funding of terrorism is obviously a very serious issue and one that requires concerted international cooperation to defeat. Statistics show a significant amount of money to fund terrorism comes from donations to charities invariably based in the Middle East and it is known that the funding would pass through many channels, including from companies, before it is in the hands of the terrorists or their arms dealers. Nevertheless, another very significant source of funding is from state actors, and you will have seen regular news reports from the USA and the European Union pointing the finger at a number of rogue nations. Indeed, there is significant friction in the Gulf States due to accusations levelled against each other of funding terrorism. Therefore, once again, cryptocurrency can be used as a medium to funnel funds to terrorists, but there is little evidence to support statements suggesting that Cryptocurrencies are a significant conduit for this.

SCAMS and Pyramid-Selling/Ponzi schemes are regularly in the news. Of course, such schemes are not new, nor unique to cryptocurrency. Sadly, there is always an element in society who seek to rip-off their fellow citizens using whatever resources are available to them. Quite often, they will be scamming close friends and even family members.

Prior to the introduction of the Internet a notorious scam in the Western World was given the name 'The Nigerian 419 Scam' and over several decades netted many millions of pounds from variously greedy/vulnerable/naïve victims; some of whom were supposedly sophisticated and worldly business folk. The arrival of the Internet allowed the scam, and many copycats, to move online and spread globally.

But perhaps the biggest scams in the world have been those in the guise of respectable multinational corporations where investors have, in some cases, lost their life savings due to the malfeasance of crooked CEOs and CFOs. Enron was the biggest in global scam in history; Bernard Madoff concocted the biggest ever Ponzi Scheme and the Lehman

Brothers Bank collapsed after fraudulent dealings by senior executives.

The key question to be addressed here is, whether Bitcoin is a scam? Bitcoin has been around now for over nine years and the interest across the world has grown exponentially. Interest not just from private individuals, but also from the big boys in Wall Street and other financial centres across the world as well as governments everywhere. Bitcoin has been subject to very intense scrutiny, probably more than any company or corporation anywhere in the world. That scrutiny is ongoing, and what is most telling is that no government has sought to outlaw Bitcoin or Cryptocurrencies. Furthermore, stock exchanges around the world are beginning to enable the trading of Bitcoin futures and Exchange Traded Funds, (ETF). Clearly these governments and institutions would not be moving ahead in this way if Bitcoin were a scam.

What has happened from time to time though, is that unscrupulous criminals have set up illegal Ponzi/Pyramid selling schemes encouraging people to invest in Bitcoin through them and promising incredible returns. Initially they manage to pay out by using the money invested by new entrants to the scheme further down the pyramid. We tend to hear about the schemes when the perpetrators are arrested by the authorities. These are not Bitcoin scams; these are scams perpetrated by criminals riding on the back of Bitcoin. It's worth repeating the sage advice, *"If it seems too good to be true, it probably is."*

A much more realistic threat to those who own Bitcoin is that of theft. Either from an online Cryptocurrency Exchange by hackers or directly from your own crypto wallet. Hacking is a very real and present danger and I'll discuss cryptocurrency exchanges in a later chapter.

Now you wouldn't leave around in public view details such as usernames and passwords for your online banking or access to your credit card accounts. You wouldn't write these details on a piece of paper and leave that paper on your work desk for any casual passer-by to see; nor would you send these details in an email or messaging system (if you do that, Stop Now!). For to do so would leave you and your family open to fraud or outright theft. By applying the same care in protecting any Bitcoin that you own you can ensure that you will not be the victim of theft. In chapter 7, Keeping Your Bitcoin Safe, I show you exactly what you need to do to protect your Bitcoin.

Chapter 5

Opportunity of a Lifetime?

Back in January 2017 I was selling my house in Hampshire and the agent brought along a young man called Dan*, he was in his early 30s and a few years earlier had suffered an accident on a building site where he was working as a labourer. He received a significant sum of money in compensation and, whether prescient or just by good luck, (I suspect the latter) invested a proportion in Bitcoin. When he came to view my house, he was already a Bitcoin millionaire - i.e. the value of his Bitcoin converted into UK pounds was in excess of £1 million.

Dan was very interested in buying my house but did not want to cash in his Bitcoins as he believed they would increase further in value. So, he was investigating alternative financing; but he was a bit of a procrastinator and we ultimately sold the house to someone else. When he viewed our house, a single Bitcoin was valued at £762; by December of the same year it had increased in value to a peak of

£14,837. Dan's Bitcoin worth had increased to nearly £20 million!

Now Dan didn't go to university In fact he hadn't undertaken any further education, having left school at 16 he went straight into work in the building trade. He wasn't knowledgeable about the world of finance or investments; in fact, when he first viewed our house it was clear he didn't fully understand how mortgages worked. It would be fair to say that Dan was an unremarkable guy, who just had the good fortune to stumble across Bitcoin at the right time; but, most importantly, saw an opportunity and took it.

I did later see him driving a new top of the range Mercedes convertible. Did he cash-in I wonder?

Clearly, there have been plenty of opportunities for investors & speculators to make incredible gains from purchasing Bitcoin. The price of Bitcoin at the time of writing has more than halved since its December 2017 peak, though nevertheless it still represents a whopping 700% increase in less than 18 months. But of course, most of you reading this are more interested in the opportunity ahead.

FOMO comes to the fore again; as many people feel they have already 'missed the boat' when it comes to Bitcoin. Whilst there is no doubt a number of people have already made a fortune from the rising valuations of Bitcoin, I'm going to show you how there is still very much more to come and we are in the very early days of this exciting Bitcoin journey.

When Satoshi Nakamoto initiated the first mining of Bitcoin he set in motion a long-term project with a finite goal of mining a maximum of 21 million Bitcoin – with 1 Bitcoin comprising 100million Satoshi (thinks cents to dollars, pence to pounds, etc). Whether cryptocurrency ultimately replaces fiat currencies, and whether that crypto is Bitcoin, no one can say for certain. However, banks and major corporations are taking this possibility very, very seriously. Some of them are taking a position of fighting against it, whilst others wish to engage with and exploit the opportunities they see ahead. So, let us assume the positive, and investigate the possible opportunity.

Bitcoin's market capitalisation, (fiat currency valuation of the mined Bitcoin to date) is about US$135 Billion, based on an approximate dollar valuation of $8,000 per Bitcoin. Now the world's total money (known as 'Broad Money') is currently valued at an equivalent of US$90 Trillion – that's $90,000,000,000,000. So, Bitcoin as a currency is an extremely small part of this – in fact 0.15%. If we extrapolate these figures and Bitcoin became accepted as a currency of use and took just 1% of Broad Money supply, then its value could reasonably increase to $53,000; if it took 10%, then $533,000. Of course, this doesn't take account of the fact that the coins are continuing to be mined which will increase supply. However, as already mentioned, there will be a maximum of 21 million Bitcoin's; 80% of which have already been mined. These figures may seem fantastical, but this is the hypothesis which is generally being used when people are forecasting potential Bitcoin prices for the future.

Just keep in mind though, there is a risk that it could bomb to zero!

You may be asking if one Bitcoin is worth $0.5 million how can people possibly use it in day-to-day transactions? Remember, one Bitcoin equals 100 million Satoshi. So, if a Bitcoin became worth the equivalent of $500,000, *one Satoshi would have an equivalent value of 1/2 a US cent.* Now you can see it would be entirely practicable to use Satoshi's and Bitcoin for day-to-day transactions.

It is very important, essential even, to consider the potential risks too. Governments across the world could collaborate to outlaw the use of Bitcoin; though I personally think this is highly unlikely. Whilst they have made a lot of noise and bluster, now they are coming to take a more considered approach, not rushing to judge. An instinct of most bureaucrats seems to be to tax where possible and they are definitely sniffing around the cryptocurrency pot, however the challenge for them is in defining and agreeing exactly what cryptocurrency is; a currency, a security, or an asset – or none of these? The other area that governments are working on is balancing the need for consumer protection without stifling innovation; a critical balance is required here.

The citizens of the world may simply not get on board with using Cryptocurrencies and prefer to stick with the historical fiat currencies; people are naturally averse to change and sometimes it takes them quite a while to accept new ways of doing things. However, once a critical mass understands the significant benefits of a safer, faster & lower transaction cost cryptocurrency system, I believe it will be unstoppable.

It's possible that another cryptocurrency may come along that's better than Bitcoin; a new kid on the block! Whilst this is possible, I think that Bitcoin as a *pure currency crypto*, enhanced by the Lightning Network, (discussed in Chapter 10), is in a very strong position to retain its prime position as the number one pure cryptocurrency. Nevertheless, it is a risk that cannot be entirely discounted.

The Catch 22 of the opportunities in Bitcoin is that the very volatility in its price set against fiat currencies, which excite so many people, can also be its Achilles Heel.

For Bitcoin to be truly successful, its price will need to stabilise and concurrently gain widespread acceptance as the currency of choice when transacting in everyday life. Whether purchasing a house, a car or just a cup of coffee; no need to even think of converting back into fiat currencies such as pounds or dollars etc. If it can achieve this, it will have met the overarching objective of its founder, Satoshi Nakamoto and become the global currency of the 21st-century.

Chapter 6

Buying, Using & Safeguarding Your Bitcoin

In deciding to enter the brave new world of Bitcoin you are also tacitly accepting that you are ***your own bank***. You are in control and with that comes responsibility. Responsibility for all of your transactions; responsibility for your own security. There is no high street bank to queue in; no call centre to play you mildly irritating music on a loop, no friendly online chat! The great thing about buying Bitcoin is that there are no upfront costs and no setup fees. There are two parts to this process:

- Setting up a Bitcoin wallet.

- Setting up an account(s) to send and receive Bitcoin.

You can have your wallet stored in a number of different places. On your PC/laptop, smart phone, on the Internet or as an off-line hardware device. I recommend you go to the official Bitcoin website,

Bitcoin.org, and you will see links to a range of reputable wallet providers.

Safeguarding your Bitcoin

Where your Bitcoin is stored, and its ease of access, is generally reflected in the level of security provided. I recommend that, for online options, you look for those that use two-stage authentication such as Google Authenticator or mobile number. I will now take you through the main options.

- Cryptocurrency Exchanges. This is where you can exchange one type of cryptocurrency for another. Generally, most Cryptocurrencies cannot be purchased with fiat money; they need to be exchanged for one of the major Cryptocurrencies, generally Bitcoin or Ether. (We will look at other Cryptocurrencies in later chapter.) The important point I wish to make here is that cryptocurrency exchanges are the least secure options for storing your Bitcoin. Exchange hosted wallets are often referred to as '*Hot Wallets*'; however, some exchanges offer the option to store your cryptocurrency off-line, in other words the ability to transfer it from *hot* to *cold* storage. Cryptocurrency exchanges are probably the least desirable place to store your cryptocurrency due to their vulnerability to hacking. Therefore, it is recommended that you just keep a minimum amount of crypto in your exchange account to enable you to make day-to-day exchange transactions if you are going to be trading regularly.

- Desktop Wallets. These are wallets that require software to be installed onto your computer; many have mobile versions too. Some wallets can be used off-line, though the majority require to be online, therefore they're are also considered '*Hot Wallets'*.

- Web-based Wallets. Similar to a desktop wallet except that no software is installed on your computer. The risk of these wallets is copycat sites set up by criminals phishing for your details, so they can steal your Bitcoin. These copycat sites purchase URLs, (website domain names), which are very similar to the authentic desktop wallet website. To protect yourself, take sensible precautions as you would for your online banking. Don't click through on links in emails, messages/texts etc, and always type in the web address manually. Good web-based

wallets will offer two-stage authentication –
so use it!

- Hardware Wallets. Sometimes referred to as
  'Cold Wallets', these offer the very best
  security currently available. These are small
  devices that look very similar to a USB stick
  but whose single function is as a
  cryptocurrency wallet. Their level of
  security is the best, as they will store your
  private keys and to access your
  cryptocurrency wallet(s) you need to open
  your hardware wallets with a PIN code. The
  key strength of the system is that your
  private keys are never revealed anywhere
  else. Importantly you must have your
  device to access your Cryptocurrencies.
  Therefore, it is vitally important that you
  secure your hardware wallet when not in
  use; for example in a house safe or maybe
  even a safety deposit box. There is a backup
  system should you lose your hardware
  wallet, which requires you to purchase a
  replacement hardware wallet and enter a
  unique set of words forming a password
  phrase (usually 20 totally random and
  disassociated words) which you will have set
  up when you activated your lost wallet. Of

course, it is essential that you store your password phrase securely in a separate location from your wallet! At the time of writing hardware wallets retail from about £90 upwards ($130, €110); so not cheap, but a worthwhile investment if you are intending to hold Cryptocurrencies in the long-term.

Once you get used to the system and processes you would probably find that you have several different wallets, for example a hardware wallet holding majority of cryptocurrency, a desktop wallet with a smaller amount for regular access and maybe an exchange wallet for day-to-day trading.

Buying your Bitcoin

So, you set up your wallets and *now you are your own bank!* Amidst the feeling of excitement at being your own bank, it's worth taking a moment for a reality check. You are the only person that can safeguard your own bank as I mentioned above. There are no government or corporate schemes in place; no protection such as the Financial Services Compensation Scheme for personal bank accounts in the UK. There is no Financial Ombudsman to complain to if something goes wrong. This is partly the reason why governments across the world are looking at ways they can regulate Cryptocurrencies and put in place safeguards for consumers; however, to date, they don't exist.

So, proceed with caution when making your first Bitcoin purchase. Remember, Bitcoin comprises 100million Satoshi's; so, it follows that you don't have to purchase whole units of Bitcoin or even a single Bitcoin. My first purchase of Bitcoin was a mere 0.25 Bitcoin back in 2013. Make your first purchase a small fraction of the Bitcoin to enable you to test and prove the process, so that should you get it wrong you don't lose much!

It doesn't automatically follow that you can purchase your Bitcoin via your wallet provider; although some do offer this service directly, others offer it indirectly through a third party. If your wallet provider does not offer a facility to purchase Bitcoin directly using fiat currency, then you will need to use one of the many online cryptocurrency brokers. Exchanges and brokers make their money by taking a very small margin of the sale; this is effectively hidden from you as it is already incorporated into the price they offer you. It's definitely worth shopping around for the best deal as there can be significant differences in the rates offered by different exchanges and brokers. Also, quite often they will offer you a different rate if paying by direct bank transfer compared to the rate if paying by debit or credit card (usually a poorer rate).

Despite the lack of government regulation, the industry is recognising their concerns and so are beginning to self-regulate. Therefore, you will find that most exchanges and brokers will restrict the level of Bitcoin purchases you can make until you have met their identity validation processes to allow you to move to a higher level of purchase. This process is commonly known as *'Know Your Customer'* – KYC. The more efficient companies can complete this process in a couple of days; however some of the less well-run companies can take several weeks. If you want to make purchases regularly, I recommend completing the KYC process as soon as possible after you first register.

Once you've registered with a broker or exchange to purchase Bitcoin it's a very straightforward transaction as follows:

- Enter the public key address of your Bitcoin wallet

- Enter the number of Bitcoin you wish to purchase

- You will be given a quote for the price in fiat currency (often with options for different ways to pay)

- Decide how you wish to pay and then accept the quote

- Make payment, either by bank transfer, debit or credit card

- As soon as the payee confirms receipt of your payment, they initiate transfer of the Bitcoin on the block chain

- Once the transaction has been validated by the minimum required number of nodes (usually six) on the Blockchain, the Bitcoin will be transferred into your wallet

- Using your private key open the wallet and you will see the Bitcoin showing as received

Dependent on how busy the Blockchain is, you may receive your Bitcoin within 10 minutes or it may take several hours. (If sending Bitcoin to another country this is still significantly quicker than transferring fiat currency).

Using your Bitcoin

I'll repeat from an earlier chapter the process for sending Bitcoin from your wallet, (and of course is reverse process for receiving)

So, say you wish to send Mrs Jones 0.5 Bitcoin; this is an example process:

- Mrs Jones advises you of her public key

- You open your encrypted Bitcoin wallet with your private key

- You enter the send Bitcoin area of your wallet and then enter Mrs Jones' public key and the amount of Bitcoin you wish to send; in this case 0.5 Bitcoin.

- You hit the submit button and the transaction is now loaded onto the Blockchain.

- Using the decentralised distributed ledger with decentralised nodes your transaction is validated by a minimum six nodes to ensure this is a valid transaction (i.e. to prevent the same Bitcoin being spent twice)

- As soon as the minimum number of nodes have validated the transaction it is confirmed on the Blockchain and Mrs Jones will see the 0.5 Bitcoin in her own encrypted Bitcoin wallet.

- The transaction is now complete.

Chapter 7

Spending It

For some, spending is fun. So, if you want to engage in retail therapy or something more ostentatious, read on.

You can already use your Bitcoin with thousands of vendors across the world. Japan and South Korea are the global leaders in enabling the consumer market for Bitcoin holders. At the end of 2017 it was estimated that there are over 10,000 businesses now accepting Bitcoin as a method of payment. In Australia you can pay your utility bills with Bitcoin. Everyday items and major purchases, ranging right up to boats and houses, have already been sold to buyers who paid using Bitcoin. Large online retailers such as Overstock.com accept Bitcoin and also global travel site, Expedia.com, as well as software giant Microsoft.

Speculation that the world's largest company, Amazon, will be accepting Bitcoin soon, continues to grow. If Amazon does accept Bitcoin, such an endorsement of its real-world utility will, I believe, fast-track the cryptocurrency's global acceptance.

In late 2017 property developer Go Homes sold two properties to buyers who paid fully in Bitcoin. A four-bedroom townhouse in Hertfordshire was bought by a Bitcoin miner and online gamer for the fiat equivalent of £595,000. They also sold a four-bedroom detached house in Colchester to another Bitcoin miner for the fiat equivalent of £350,000. The UK Government's official Land Registry is now permitting property sale prices to be recorded in Bitcoin.

In London, a property investment company director has placed his home on the market at the fiat equivalent of £17 million however, in an effort to spur the widespread acceptance of Bitcoin, he is only accepting the cryptocurrency as payment.

Where old meets new! How about a pair of giant mammoth tusks? These beasts from the Ice Age can be yours for about 17 BTC (at time of writing) and are being sold by Canadian, Richard Marcus of Vancouver.

From Ice Age to Space Age. Sir Richard Branson's Virgin Galactic is accepting Bitcoin for those who wish to book and become the world's first space tourists. This really captures my imagination, I would love to do this, so had better start saving as the price is about 25 BTC at current rates; I wonder if that includes meals?

A couple of websites can help you identify online and local businesses accepting Bitcoin for more prosaic items. The website spendabit.co is effectively a consumer facing website that aggregates a huge range of items for sale from a cross-section of retailers. Using their scalable map, Coinmap.org will help you find local businesses across the world accepting Bitcoin.

The physical process of spending Bitcoin is dependent on whether you are undertaking an online transaction or a bricks and mortar/face-to-face transaction. An online transaction will follow the similar process to that already outlined in the previous chapter the sending Bitcoin to another person.

A bricks and mortar/face-to-face transaction could follow the same process as online. However, if you have a mobile Bitcoin wallet then the transaction could be as simple as scanning the vendors QR code and then confirming the amount you wish to send.

My Bitcoin QR code

Spending is a necessary part of everyday life. By spending Bitcoin you are doing your bit in helping it gain global acceptance.

Chapter 8

Cashing In

There is a tendency for some Bitcoin holders to become overly focused on the fiat value of their Bitcoin. With all the media hype and sensationalism this is understandable; however, think about why you are buying your Bitcoin in the first place. Are you a:

- Speculator

- Investor

- True believer of the new world order

If you are a speculator, then it is understandable why you may be keenly following the day-to-day movements of the fiat price of Bitcoin. You are clearly speculating that the fiat price is going to zoom onwards and upwards, and presumably as quickly as possible. I just hope you have your helmet on and are strapped in for this particularly exhilarating ride; as the cryptocurrency market, in its infancy, is extremely volatile unlike anything you will have experienced before. Therefore, as much as you may be anticipating spectacular gains you have to be prepared for gravity defying drops. I hope you have the stomach for it? Good luck!

If you are an investor, after reading this book you will continue your due diligence and, having decided to invest, will appreciate the long-term potential whilst accepting that, hand-in-hand with possible historic record beating gains, like other Cryptocurrencies, Bitcoin carries the risk to crash to zero.

When you do decide to cash in your Bitcoin into fiat currency, the process is simply a replication of the purchase process substituting your public key for the buyer's public key you will be sending Bitcoin to.

A true believer of the new world order - if this matches your approach to Bitcoin - then you are in step with Satoshi Nakamoto.

The vision of Satoshi Nakamoto is for you to use Bitcoin in your everyday life. If it realises its potential, then of course you have the opportunity for some astronomical gains in the value of your Bitcoin. Potentially, whilst one Bitcoin might enable you to purchase a good quality second-hand car today, in 10 years' time it might enable you to purchase a very fine home for your family.

Chapter 9

Your Entry Pass to The Ubiquitous Universe of Altcoins

Altcoins is the term originally used by Bitcoin purists to describe other Cryptocurrencies than Bitcoin itself; meaning *'alternative coins'*. It has now become a commonly used term within the cryptocurrency community; however, the general public still tend to refer to Cryptocurrencies.

At the time of writing there are now over 1600 Altcoins in virtual circulation across the world. While a small number of Altcoins can be purchased direct from a broker using fiat currency paying by bank transfer or use of a credit/debit card, most of them have to be obtained via Cryptocurrency Exchanges.

The exchanges enable you to obtain Altcoins by trading them with a handful of the top Cryptocurrencies by market capitalisation. It follows therefore that you must already own some Cryptocurrencies to enable you to trade. Bitcoin is the number one cryptocurrency by market capitalisation, it is the premier cryptocurrency, the *'Daddy of Cryptocurrencies'.* Consequently, Bitcoin is tradable with just about every Altcoin on every exchange across the world.

So, if you want to engage in the wider cryptocurrency markets, Bitcoin is your entry pass.

Chapter 10

Developments in Bitcoin

One of the most fascinating facts about Bitcoin and possibly one of the hardest for people to accept is that no entity controls Bitcoin. No organisation or company or individual. Not even its creator Satoshi Nakamoto; and that's exactly what he intended. Any decisions about the future of Bitcoin must be agreed by a majority consensus of Bitcoin users.

Software developers are constantly looking at ways to improve Bitcoin. To put into effect any improvements they have to achieve a majority consensus; if they achieve this consensus they make the change. However, if they do not achieve a consensus, but still wish to make the change, they need to initiate what is known as a hard fork. A hard fork is when a fundamental change is made to the software of Bitcoin without a consensus and so a new modified version of Bitcoin becomes available. In this scenario all Bitcoin holders will be airdropped, (given), a certain number of the modified version of Bitcoin; and it will have a new name. This has already occurred twice in the past 18 months; which is why we now have Bitcoin Cash (BCH) and Bitcoin Gold (BTG).

There are some very clear and readily identifiable areas for improvement on which consensus has been agreed but the solution is still being worked on.

One such area is the speed of processing transactions, known as the hash rate. Currently the number of transactions processed per second on the Bitcoin Blockchain averages about seven. To put this in perspective transactions processed per second globally by the Visa credit card network is 24,000. Clearly Bitcoin needs to match this and ideally exceed it. Work is ongoing to upgrade the transaction rate using a process known as *Lightning Network*.

The Lightning Network is a much anticipated upgrade to Bitcoin's functionality. It is being developed independently and is designed to be layered over bitcoin, (it is also intended to deliver similar improved functionality to a cryptocurrency called Litecoin). For those of you who are familiar with websites, an analogy for the Lightning Network is as follows:

Internet equates to the Blockchain as the enabling technology.

Websites hosted on the Internet equate to bitcoin operating on the Internet.

Widgets on the website equate to the Lightning Network enabling enhanced functionality.

The technology is still in the beta stage, (developing, testing & improving). However, it is rumoured to be very close to full mainnet, (full network as opposed to a test network) release.

An additional benefit of the Lightning Network is the ability to undertake Atomic Swaps. This has already been tested and proven at the beta stage and if implemented for Bitcoin will be an enhancement of significant magnitude. Essentially an Atomic Swap enables transactions between different cryptocurrencies without an intermediary; for example, a cryptocurrency exchange. Consequently, transactions could take place with one party paying with Bitcoin and the other receiving Ethereum in payment. Imagine in our current fiat payment system purchasing something in the USA, but sending pounds in payment and the seller receiving dollars without the transaction going through any third parties, such as a bank or credit card processor. Clearly, this is incredibly complicated but exciting and real *'reach for the stars'* project. If this is implemented it will further speed up transactions, reduce costs significantly and by cutting out an intermediary, further enhance security.

Once the Lightning Network is implemented for Bitcoin it will be a quantum leap forward for the cryptocurrency to becoming the universally accepted form of payment.

Chapter 11

The Myth of the Man

A global *urban myth* has developed around the name Satoshi Nakamoto. Unlike so many inventors, scientists, innovators and entrepreneurs throughout history, Satoshi Nakamoto has purposely elected to remain in the shadows of his world-changing innovation. In doing so, he has elevated the level of interest and speculation surrounding him to a global scale.

Crypto enthusiasts, amateur sleuths and the media have all speculated as to who Nakamoto really is. Is Nakamoto a 'he', or a 'she' or even a group of people? As Nakamoto has chosen a male nomenclature, I will refer to him as 'he'.

The few clues that Nakamoto conspicuously left takes us both East and West. The nomme de guerre that is used points to a Japanese nationality. However, a line that he left in the code when initiating bitcoin seem to indicate either a British citizen or residency in the UK. On the face of it, it seems unlikely that somebody outside of the UK would have selected a headline from a British newspaper; as follows:

"The Times 03/Jan/2009 Chancellor on brink of second bailout for banks"

Of course, this may have been a deliberate red herring.

After initiating bitcoin in 2009, Nakamoto continued to develop it with other online developers, but none of them met him face-to-face or even spoke to him via any medium. The only way he communicated was via email. In the mid-2010 he handed over control to some key personnel in the bitcoin.org circle and has not been heard of since.

Various individuals in the cryptocurrency world have been identified as potentially being Satoshi Nakamoto but in every case the evidence cited was circumstantial rather than compelling. Newsweek magazine believed they had uncovered the identity of Nakamoto having found a retired engineer with the same surname enjoying a quiet retirement in California. It resulted in quite a media circus descending on a clearly very perplexed and confused Dorian Nakamoto and it didn't take long for it to become clear that Newsweek had made some rather outlandish assumptions when compiling their exclusive.

A pretender to the Crown, has stepped into the limelight claiming to be Satoshi Nakamoto; an Australian named Craig Wright. The only person to have made this claim, which he states he had been pressurised into making by business partners. Whether he is merely an opportunist or not, the consensus is that it is unlikely that he is Nakamoto. Having seen recorded interviews with him, my view of the sort of character that he appears to be, it would seem unlikely that he is the individual who is taking the course of action outlined below.

A more prosaic reason why Nakamoto may have chosen to remain anonymous is that in the initial mining, he personally mined 1 million bitcoins. So, if one bitcoin is valued at $10,000, his holding would be worth $10 billion; making him one of the richest men in the world. However, intriguingly the Blockchain shows that he has not cashed in any of his bitcoin. Perhaps he has died, or maybe he is a genuinely altruistic man whose main drive was to improve the lot for his fellow man.

As Satoshi Nakamoto is no longer involved in the ongoing development of bitcoin, the importance of his identity is more of a desire to satisfy curiosity.

Nevertheless, his substantial holding of bitcoin ensures that he still has potential to impact it. Should he decide to cash-in a significant number of his bitcoin, it would surely impact on its fiat value. The past decade of inaction may well indicate no intent to do so; however, it cannot be conclusively ruled out.

Whilst he did not develop the Blockchain itself, he was the first to take the huge leap of faith in developing the world's first cryptocurrency. An innovation that jumpstarted a new age of technological advances with unprecedented potential to improve so many aspects of people's lives, business and even democracy itself.

Personally, I hope that if his identity ever became known, he would be nominated for the Nobel Prize.

Section 2

Chapter 12

The Wonderful World of Cryptocurrencies & Blockchain

Whether Bitcoin realises its potential and becomes the global currency or whether it crashes to zero I have absolutely no idea. And don't believe anybody else who tells you they know otherwise. But what I can be sure of is that the underlying Blockchain technology is a disruptive technology that is set to change the way so many industries do business and is here to stay for the foreseeable future; that is until overtaken by the next technological leap forward.

Cryptocurrencies are a bit like the visible part of the iceberg which is the part of the Blockchain technology visible to the public. At the time of writing, current valuations of the whole cryptocurrency markets equates to around $300 billion. However, Blockchain technology is much more than just the Cryptocurrencies which are effectively a side-product of that technology, a financial source that is used to pay to power it. Whilst the cryptocurrency market may have a valuation of around $300 billion I would hazard a guess that the Blockchain technology industry is already valued in the trillions of dollars as so many banks, industries and even governments are secretly developing their own uses for Blockchain which will in effect be private.

Already we are seeing governmental and non-governmental organisations using the Blockchain technology today. The following, amongst others, are declared trialling/using:

International Union for Conservation of Nature

Papa New Guinea, for cross-border transactions

Republic of Georgia, for land title registration

State of Andhra Pradesh, India, for land title registration

State of Virginia, USA, for state elections

UNICEF

United Nations, for food aid distribution

US Department of Defence, for weapons management

Many, many companies are conducting trials with Blockchain technology. Some of the biggest ones include:

Allianz insurance

Amazon

Barclays Bank

BMW, Ford, Renault, General Motors

British Airways

Co-op

IBM

Maersk Shipping

Walmart

As you can see from this quick sample list it touches just about all industries. I give you this sample list to help you understand the real global scalability and network capability of Blockchain and consequently cryptocurrencies. Many of these Blockchains will be privately owned and run; however many will be public and that is where the cryptocurrency opportunities will be.

Now to date there are over 1600 Cryptocurrencies available across the world. Of those, consensus is that many will fail. Either because they are outright scams, don't solve a problem in a better way, (in other words they just jumped on the cryptocurrency bandwagon), have poor management teams or simply don't have real global scalability and network capability. Nevertheless, within that 1600 there will be some real gems which will be bringing significant benefits in solving a problem or improving on a service or product.

It is important, at this point, that you understand that the term of cryptocurrencies is a rather generic term. Personally, I think it's rather misleading. The majority of the cryptocurrencies available now are not currencies in the same sense that Bitcoin is, although some are. In other words, they cannot be used to purchase goods. The whole premise of Bitcoin is that it will become a global currency to replace fiat currencies. Of course, it remains to be seen whether it achieves that.

Many cryptocurrencies are effectively tokens who sole purpose is to facilitate the transaction on the Blockchain on which it is based. Rather like the tokens that you buy in amusement arcades and fairgrounds. You might buy £10 worth of tokens, for which you receive 20 tokens and then use one of those tokens each time you take a ride on a roller-coaster or bumper-cars. You can't use those tokens anywhere else, for example to buy your fish & chips or to take the bus home. You may be able to cash the unused ones in with the fairground management or perhaps you might be able to sell a few to another member of the public in the fairground.

Say you had a cryptocurrency called LawCoin issued by GlobalLawyers. Your cryptocurrency might, for example, enable you to draw up your Last Will & Testament which will be validated and stored on a legal services Blockchain, until you either cancel it, amend it or die. In any of those instances the action taken will be immediately recorded on the Blockchain. And if you die, the Will is automatically released to your Executors. For your use of that service, you would pay a cryptocurrency charge, automatically triggered when certain actions are completed, for example when the Will is notarised. So, you can see from this example that you would be using your cryptocurrency in a real-world situation.

You may have bought a number of LawCoin simply as an investment. Presuming you did your due diligence and GlobalLawyers became the number one global provider of Blockchain based Wills, then it is possible that the value of your LawCoin will have increased and you may decide to cash out by either trading it with Bitcoin, some other cryptocurrency or a fiat currency.

Conversely there are other Cryptocurrencies that have been developed to be a real-world currency like Bitcoin.

When we look back to the early days of the Internet, the boom days, there were many companies listing on stock exchanges which were given astronomical values based on nothing more than having a website and not much else. Come the crash of the early 2000 those companies went under and what arose from the ashes, Phoenix like, were the Internet giants that we know today such as Google, Amazon, Netflix, AliBaba, Facebook, Twitter and YouTube to name just a few. This will likely be the scenario with cryptocurrencies.

If you decide to enter the brave new world of cryptocurrencies it is fundamental that you understand what they are about. Do your due diligence. There are a few key questions that should be answered to your satisfaction, so you can understand the level of risk before you purchase/invest in a cryptocurrency.

What real-world problem is it a solution for? Is it really a better way of dealing with the issue than the current approach?

Who are the team behind it? Don't be swayed by celebrity endorsements. In fact, if they need a celebrity endorsement it should raise a red flag. Check that the team shown on the website are in fact real people, (scammers have been known to put false identities on the sites). Check their LinkedIn profiles.

Where are they in terms of the timeline for the development of the underlying technology on which the cryptocurrency is based? In some of the scam cases it's got no further than being an idea! Have they already received institutional funding if so from whom and can you verify that?

What is the realistic potential in global scalability and network? Not easy to assess, but you need to think about this if you are looking at the cryptocurrency being an investment.

These are not easy factors to assess, but it is important that you do so. There are many online forums, where the merits of cryptocurrencies are discussed, and it is worth looking at a few of these to try to gain a feel for the consensus. Be warned though, do not follow through on any cryptocurrency purchase based on a forum recommendation alone, as there are many sharks out there seeking to boost the cryptocurrency for their own benefit often for what is known as a *Pump and Dump* scam.

Pump & Dump

Pump & Dump is a process that has been around for decades, possibly even hundreds of years. It's a particularly pernicious practice that unscrupulous speculators have used extensively in the stocks and shares markets around the world; although today the various regulatory authorities keep a sharp lookout for any signs of such practices. Some pyramid selling/Ponzi schemes have also used Pump & Dump.

Essentially the *'pump'* is achieved by circulating misleading/false statements about a product or share over a period of time to give the impression that the product or share is currently undervalued and would imminently skyrocket in price. In the Victorian period this would be achieved through the careful placing of so-called insider information with naïve individuals who will in turn spread the information. During the Victorian period, the process would take some time due to the limitations of communication. Now in the 21st-century, one of the favourite mediums is social media; Facebook, Twitter, chat forums, even YouTube to name a few. As the product or share is continually pumped so it's value inflates in the same way as a balloon is pumped up. As less sophisticated investors (or punters?) see the value increasing the whole process becomes a self-perpetuating myth and more and more people pile-in not wishing to miss out on the amazing opportunity.

The architects of the Pump & Dump scheme would have got in at ground level. They will have either bought a significant number of shares or products at the lowest price, prior to the pumping commencing.

When the architects of the pump and dump scheme calculate that they have either sucked in as many unsuspecting punters as possible and/or the price of the shares of product has peaked they will sell, '*dump*', their shares or products to a final group of naïve investors and make off with their huge profits made, based on nothing more than speculative rumour-mongering. They will cease their pumping operation and consequently an awareness will grow that the shares or product have been grossly overvalued and so the price will fall off a cliff and many, many people would have lost an awful lot of money. So often, those who lose money are those who can least afford to.

That these Pump & Dump schemes still succeed today is because so many people are desperate to believe the hype and find a way to make some easy money. The often-repeated adage, "If *it seems too good to be true, it probably is.*", is worth heeding.

Criminals and scammers are always on the lookout for a new way to fleece people of their hard-earnt money. Sadly, the cryptocurrency world has attracted a significant number of them and the news headlines regularly report on the latest one exposed, sometimes too late to prevent people losing money.

The most common format for the criminals and scammers is through what is known as an initial coin offering, ICO. Whereas in the past a company might seek to raise funds through the stock market, or in the past decade through crowdfunding, a new route is through the ICO. Now this is a legitimate route for a company that has a real Blockchain based business and if you do your due diligence, as discussed above, you will quickly see which businesses are legitimate.

An ICO is a way for a business to raise funds to (further) develop their Blockchain innovation. They do this by offering their cryptocurrency coins/tokens for sale to institutions and the general public. Usually there are a finite number of coins available and once sold they usually become tradable. It's important to understand that when buying a cryptocurrency through an ICO you are not buying a share of the business; you are just buying that cryptocurrency only. Normally the purpose of the cryptocurrency is rather like a payment system to utilise whatever the Blockchain technology is. It is sometimes likened to a fuel that is powering the system. Now should the Blockchain technology gain widespread use, market forces will generally ensure the fiat value of its related cryptocurrency will increase and this is where investors will see a return on their investment.

It is quite easy to create your own cryptocurrency. Even if you don't have the technical competence you can hire somebody who does relatively inexpensively. Scammers and criminals have seen this as an easy route to riches and have been designing cryptocurrencies based on the flimsiest and most expedient ideas, set up a website and then initiate their ICO. Remember, there is currently no regulatory authority to police this; (although law enforcement agencies are now monitoring this area closely, and where there is a clear breach of existing laws are taking action to close it down). Once scammers have got their ICO up and running they use the full range of online and social media marketing methods to promote and pump up their cryptocurrency. Helped by FOMO, the ICO's have tended to sell out and then be pumped up to give rapid increases in value, sometimes of thousands of percent before the scammers then bail out causing the value to drop like a stone never to recover.

I write this not to scare you, but to ensure that you fully understand how much of a *Wild West* the cryptocurrency world currently is and so to help you manage the risks. I won't apologise for saying this again; if you do your due diligence then you will identify cryptocurrencies that truly have the potential to change the world and reward you with exponential returns on your investment.

Whilst it may be the Wild West, the Sheriff is coming to town. Once there is a semblance of law and order and clear regulatory standards then the really *big money* will start to enter the cryptocurrency markets. By *big money* I mean pension funds, hedge funds, mutual funds, etc whose investments tend to start in the tens of millions of dollars. Once these huge financial institutions start investing directly in the Blockchain technology and their cryptocurrencies it is clear that those with real world scalability and network potential will see their valuations skyrocket. Therefore, in my opinion, for those willing to take the risk that they could lose all their money, there is nevertheless huge opportunity.

BUGS, HACKERS & HACKATHONS

Hardly a week passes without a newspaper headline screaming out that a cryptocurrency or crypto exchange has been hacked and the equivalent of millions of dollars of cryptocurrency stolen. If you have taken appropriate measures to secure your own cryptocurrency you are unlikely to be affected. However, sometimes you may be unlucky and get caught up in a hack. Any cryptocurrency exchange that wishes to retain its customers and its business ensures that it covers any losses. Whilst these hacks often result in the loss of millions of dollars of crypto, the exchanges are generally making such phenomenal profits that they can afford to cover the loss. For example, the largest cryptocurrency exchange in the world, Binance, made profits in excess of $200 million in the first quarter 2018. This upstart business's profits exceeded those of the German Deutsche Bank which has been in existence for nearly 150 years!

Notwithstanding their huge profits, cryptocurrency exchanges and block chain technology companies obviously don't want to be hacked. Despite employing the best and brightest brains on the planet sometimes a bug, (error), in the code goes unnoticed during development. A bug causing a small glitch, to a hacker, is like leaving the doors to the vault open. Sadly, some of the best and brightest brains are also hackers!

To counter this, it is becoming increasingly common for cryptocurrency exchanges and companies launching ICO's to initiate what has become known as Hackathons. Essentially, operated rather like a competition, it's an opportunity for coders to read through the software code and identify any bugs. The reward for identifying such bugs is commensurate to the potential damage that could have resulted should the bug have remained. It is not unusual to see payments of up to $10,000 for identifying a single bug. The fact the rewards are so good, means that for some coders Hackathons have effectively become their form of self-employment. The bottom line is that for the companies a Hackathon is a worthwhile investment, so don't be alarmed when you see a Hackathon advertised on the website promoting its own ICO.

In the next five chapters I will give you an overview of the Top 5 Cryptocurrencies (after Bitcoin which is number 1) by market capitalisation.

Chapter 13

 Ether (ETH)

Ether is the second largest cryptocurrency by market capitalization after Bitcoin making it the second most invested cryptocurrency in the world.

What are Ether & Ethereum?

Many people confuse Ether with Ethereum or use them interchangeably. However, they are interdependent.

Ethereum is a network or platform consisting of computers around the globe (distributed) based on the Blockchain technology. The network is always available with virtually no possibility of downtime. Free from censorship it is not controlled by any governing body. The network enables and supports smart contracts — applications programmed for a variety of purposes. The applications allow creation, storage, and transfer of sensitive data like financial transactions, contracts, or wills in a secure fashion.

Ether (Symbol: ETH) is the cryptocurrency that fuels the Ethereum network. It is used to pay for the resources used and the transactions committed on the Ethereum network. Ether is transferred from one account to another on the Ethereum platform.

Why is Ethereum needed?

Ethereum was primarily designed to overcome one limitation of Bitcoin at that time — the lack of scripting language. Its proposer, Vitalik Buterin, had voiced that Bitcoin needed a scripting language to extend its Blockchain functionality beyond currency transfer. The inclusion of a scripting language would allow development of applications that utilize its Blockchain for different purposes.

Simply put, the Bitcoin Blockchain gave users a set of pre-defined operations that performed a limited number of functions when executed. These operations were primarily designed to transfer

Bitcoins or other Cryptocurrencies. Ethereum Blockchain, on the other hand, would give users the freedom of creating their own set of operations allowing them to leverage the power of Blockchain for different applications.

History of Ethereum

> ➢ Ethereum was envisioned by Vitalik Buterin in 2013 followed by the publishing of a White Paper that described the technical design and architecture of Ethereum.
> ➢ Ethereum was announced officially in January 2014 at the North American Bitcoin Conference in the USA.
> ➢ Dr. Gavin Wood, co-founder of Ethereum, published the Ethereum Yellow Paper in April 2014 detailing technical specifications for Ethereum Virtual Machine (EVM).
> ➢ The Ethereum Foundation (Stiftung Ethereum) was established in June 2014.
> ➢ A crowdfunding campaign took place in July and August 2014 for financing the project. A presale of Ether tokens was conducted which raised over $18 million.
> ➢ Ethereum Frontier network went live on 30 July 2015.

- The Decentralized Autonomous Organization (DAO) was introduced in June 2016.
- In 2017 The Enterprise Ethereum Alliance (EEA) was founded by thirty prominent companies. Its membership increased to over 150 by July 2017.
- Ether experienced a 13,000% increase in value to January 2018.

Ethereum Blockchain

The Ethereum Blockchain consists of many nodes across the globe connected to the same network. A node is simply a computer that is a part of the Ethereum network. The network consists of many such computers that form its backbone. The nodes may be owned individually or by organizations. Any user with a computer can enlist it as a node by downloading and installing the Ethereum client software on it (hence they are also called clients). The nodes collectively maintain and update the Blockchain data.

Each node runs the Ethereum Virtual Machine (EVM), which is responsible for the execution of transactions and smart contracts. Consider your laptop as an example. It has an operating system like

Windows or Macintosh or Linux, which runs different applications. These applications may include a media player for songs or videos or a word processor for writing text documents. Similarly, an EVM is the framework or operating system for the Ethereum network. It allows different applications to run on the Ethereum network. The EVM includes a Blockchain database known as a Distributed Ledger that has information like account balances and transactions. Think of the database like a bank's ledger with records of its account holders, but it is not held in a central location. Instead it is decentralised on the Distributed Ledger held on nodes.

There are two types of nodes – full nodes and light nodes.

A full node verifies each transaction of every block. A block is a group of transactions. The node ensures that each transaction follows the rules of the network. If Rebbeca wants to send Sophie 100 Ether, a full node will first verify that Rebecca's account has 100 Ether. If Rebecca's account does not have the required Ether, the full node will invalidate the transaction and the block containing it. A full node may have the entire Blockchain database. Full nodes require significant computing resources.

Light nodes do not have the entire Blockchain database and can't verify every transaction of every block. They rely on full nodes for providing them the missing information. Consider the same transaction wherein Rebecca wants to send Sophie 100 Ether. It is received by a light node that doesn't know if Rebecca's account has the requisite funds. The node will then ask a full node if Rebecca's account has the funds. If the full node confirms the same, the light node will then mark the transaction as valid. Light nodes can run on devices with low computing power.

The Ethereum network will continue to run even if one or more nodes go offline. Even though this method creates redundancy and is less efficient than a centralized server maintaining a database, it provides an uncensored and decentralized network that has virtually zero downtime and consequently immune to outages.

Ethereum Smart Contracts

If two individuals or organizations wanted to trade with each other, they would traditionally go to a law firm for drawing up a trade agreement. The law firm would charge them a fee for drawing up the agreement and managing it on a continuous basis. Smart contracts on the Ethereum network allow the creation of the same agreement without the need for an intermediary.

Let's say Alan wants to hire Bob for developing a website. Bob will charge Alan $700 for the website. They both specify these terms in the smart contract. Alan will concurrently buy Ether worth $700 which will act as a guarantee. The Ether bought will be locked under the smart contract. As soon as Bob develops and deploys the website for Alan, the smart contract will be updated. The Ether locked under the contract will be transferred to Bob, who can then convert it into $700. It leads to completion of the smart contract. What if Bob is not able to deliver the website to Alan? In such a scenario the contract will be terminated and the Ether locked under the contract will be refunded to Alan.

This is an oversimplification of how the smart contracts work. The Ethereum network eliminates the need for third parties like law firms, banks, and auditing agencies.

An Ethereum Wallet is used to store and transfer Ether. A regular Ethereum wallet only sends and receives Ether while an Ethereum Smart Wallet also supports smart contract functionality. Those who only need to trade Ether can use a regular Ethereum wallet.

Ethereum's Proof of Work Algorithm

The nodes in the Ethereum network can also act as mining machines. Mining is simply a process of receiving, verifying and executing transactions on the Ethereum Blockchain while securing the network. Mining also issues new Ether coins to miners. A miner is the owner of a mining node. Miners dedicate their computer hardware to the Ethereum network for executing transactions, verifying them and adding them to the Blockchain. They also incur electricity bills for running their nodes. Miners receive Ether coins as a reward for their contributions to the network.

There are different types of algorithms used for verifying and executing the transactions. Ethereum uses Ethash *Proof of Work* algorithm. In this method, the mining nodes on the network receive the transactions that have to be verified and executed. The mining nodes receive multiple transactions at a time. They execute the transactions and group them into sets called blocks. Each block consists of multiple transactions that will update various accounts on the network. The Ethereum Blockchain contains information regarding the accounts and maintains immutable records of all transactions on the network.

So let's consider ten unconnected individuals who want to send Ether from their accounts to other individuals.

Ether will have to be debited from the accounts of the senders and credited to the accounts of the recipients. Then the Ethereum Blockchain database must be updated to reflect these changes. Every node on the network will receive these transactions. Each mining node will verify and execute these ten transactions and group them into a block. Multiple mining nodes across the globe create blocks simultaneously. Mining nodes compete with one another so that their block is the next one to be added to the Blockchain. The mining node whose block is added to the Blockchain first receives a small amount of Ether in reward.

As execution of instructions or smart contracts consumes resources like computing power and memory, the network users have to pay a very small fee in Ether for the same.

The Ethereum network also supports non-mining nodes. There is no incentive provided for running a non-mining Ethereum node. Developers, enthusiasts, and currency exchanges are a few parties that might operate non-mining nodes.

Ethereum's Switch to Proof of Stake

Vitalik Buterin announced plans to shift Ethereum from a Proof of Work to a Proof of Stake network, known as 'Casper'. A Proof of Stake system verifies and executes transactions differently from a Proof of Work system. The primary purpose of this is to reduce the amount of electricity consumed for sustaining the Blockchain network. It also aims to minimize the risk of centralization and improve security. Additionally, a concept called *sharding* is being developed to improve the network speed by processing multiple transactions in parallel.

While the Proof of Work system has miners, a Proof of Stake system has *forgers*. Both miners and forgers process and verify transactions. However, there are a few differences.

Miners compete with each other to get their block added first to the Blockchain. Miners are awarded Ether for every block they add successfully to the Blockchain which is known as the block reward. Any individual having a computer with the EVM client can become a miner.

Forgers, on the other hand, are chosen deterministically. A Proof of Stake system does not offer block rewards. Instead, the forgers receive a part of the transactions fees charged to the network users as a reward for their contribution.

When the Proof of Stake algorithm is implemented, a validator pool will be created. The pool will comprise of individuals who want to become forgers. There will be no priority system to select forgers. Instead, they will be selected based on the current Ether coins they own. There can be an infinite number of forgers at a given time. However, the reimbursement they receive will also increase or decrease depending on their numbers. The Casper protocol will require a forger to deposit Ether as security before being allowed to operate. If the forger commits a violation, they will lose their entire deposit.

Industry experts are skeptical regarding the proof of stake algorithm and miners across the globe are voicing discontent over the implementation as they believe it will reduce the rewards for the participating nodes. At the time of writing, there is no official date regarding the implementation of the Casper protocol.

Ethereum Controversies

Ethereum has been the centre of many controversies. These are some of the major issues.

Decentralized Autonomous Contracts (DAO) – The DAO was a venture capital fund built on the Ethereum Blockchain that was primarily meant to showcase a decentralized business model based on Ethereum. It was launched on 30 April 2016 and had a value of over US$150 million on 21 May 2016. The fund was hacked on 16 June 2016 via vulnerabilities in the system, leading to a loss of over $50 million. The hack was later reversed using a hard fork and security vulnerabilities were addressed. However, it divided the Ethereum community and led to the separation of the Ethereum into two Blockchains – Ethereum and Ethereum Classic.

Parity Vulnerabilities – Parity is a company that issues smart contracts for users of the Ethereum network. In November 2016, a junior developer accidentally deleted a function of the smart contract due to a security vulnerability. The deletion of the function disabled the transfer of Ether locked under the contract rendering it effectively useless and inaccessible. The amount of Ether in the contract was estimated to be over $150 million. Parity decided not to fork the Ethereum Blockchain after the majority of the users voted against it in April 2018. The company also stated via a blog post that they are working on Ethereum Improvement Proposals (EIP) to find alternate ways to unblock the funds. Parity had previously been subjected to another hack in July of the same year when a bug in their wallet was exploited to steal Ether valued at $31 million. Parity has addressed all security vulnerabilities that led to the hacks.

How to Purchase and Trade Ether?

Ether is sold and traded at different cryptocurrency exchanges around the globe. Users can register on these exchanges and trade Ether and other currencies. The exchanges might require the users to undergo verification processes before they can start trading. The most popular cryptocurrency exchanges include:

- Binance (Worldwide)
- Coinbase (Worldwide)
- OKEx (World Wide)
- Huub (Worldwide)
- Bitfinex (Hong Kong)
- Upbit (South Korea)
- Kraken (USA)
- Bitstamp (UK)
- Bittrex (USA)

Ether can be bought using fiat currencies, credit cards, and debit cards depending on the regulations of the country of purchase and the medium of purchase.

> **Bitcoins** – Ether can be purchased with Bitcoins from almost every cryptocurrency exchange.
> **Fiat Currencies** – Some currency exchanges allow users to purchase Ether with fiat currencies like Dollars, Pounds or Euros.
> **Altcoins** – Ether can be purchased using many altcoins.
> **Credit and Debit Cards** – Ether can be purchased using debit and credit cards. Some countries or exchanges might not allow credit cards for purchasing Cryptocurrencies.

It is important to get an Ethereum wallet before purchasing Ether. Just as a regular wallet is required to store printed fiat currencies, an Ethereum wallet is used to store Ether. Both software and hardware wallets are available for storing Ether.

Summarising Ethereum

> Ethereum is a decentralized global network based on the Blockchain technology.

- Ether is the currency used on the Ethereum network for processing transactions and paying fees for them.
- Ethereum supports scripting languages that extend its functionalities beyond currency transfer.
- The network consists of nodes that run the Ethereum Virtual Machine (EVM). Anyone with a computer can enlist as a node.
- Ethereum allows the creation of Smart Contracts that are a digital form of trade agreements between entities who want to conduct business.
- Ethereum makes use of mining for verifying and processing transactions. The process involves computation of complex mathematical equations.
- Individuals and organizations around the globe can enlist as mining nodes with Ethereum. They compete with each other to get their block of transactions added to the Ethereum ledger. Miners receive Ether as reimbursement for dedicating their resources to the network.

- ➤ Planned upgrade from Proof of Work to Proof of Stake will significantly enhance efficiency and speed of Ethereum.
- ➤ Most prominent cryptocurrency exchanges around the globe sell Ether.

Ether Quick Stats

Issue Date: July 2014 (pre-sale).

Can be Mined: Yes

Issue Price: $0.311 (1BTC = 2000 Ether)

Peak Fiat Price to Date: $1,448.18 – 13 Jan 2018.

Market Cap: $60,440,708,898 – 8 June 2018.

Circulating Supply: 99,940,488 ETH – 8 June 2018.

Available/Total Supply: 99.9 Million

Website: https://www.ethereum.org

Chapter 14

 Ripple (XRP)

Ripple is the third largest cryptocurrency by market capitalization after Bitcoin and Ethereum making it the third most invested cryptocurrency in the world.

What are Ripple and XRP?

Ripple and XRP are two different yet interdependent terms though most people use them interchangeably.

Ripple, formally RippleNet, is a global financial network based on the Blockchain technology. It is a decentralized network founded upon the distributed Ripple payment protocol that defines the rules governing the network. The network can transfer tokens that may represent fiat currencies, Cryptocurrencies, and even commodities. Various banks, financial institutions, and payment providers are part of the RippleNet. It is used for processing and clearing financial transactions and has support for real-time messaging.

XRP is a token or a cryptocurrency used in the Ripple network. It can be transferred from one account to another as well as exchanged for fiat currencies like Dollars, Pound or Euros, commodities like gold and other units of value like smartphone talk time.

Why is Ripple needed?

Ripple was born out of the need for a decentralized monetary system that allowed the creation of independent currencies. Jed McCaleb who conceived the idea for the Ripple network wanted to develop a system that did not rely on mining like Bitcoin. Bitcoin uses mining to process the transactions. The process involves solving complex mathematical equations for verifying transactions which take time and consume a large amount of electricity. Ripple has been developed to perform transactions faster than Bitcoin while lowering electricity consumption. It uses the consensus protocol for accomplishing the same. Ripple also eliminates the need for centralized exchanges, unlike Bitcoin. The Ripple network itself can be used to interchange fiat currencies and Cryptocurrencies.

History of Ripple

- ➢ Ryan Fugger develops the Ripplepay protocol in 2004.
- ➢ Ripplepay.com was launched in 2005 and offered secure payment services to an online community with members from across the globe.
- ➢ In 2011 Jed McCaleb came up with the idea of a cryptocurrency that does not use mining like Bitcoin for verifying transactions but relies on the agreement of participating nodes. He starts developing the new system along with Arthur Britto and David Schwartz.
- ➢ Chris Larsen, the founder of E-Loan and Prosper, joined the team in August 2012 and with Jed McCaleb they take the idea to Ryan Fugger who also joins.
- ➢ OpenCoin Inc. is formed in September 2012 to oversee the development of the project. Work begins on the Ripple Transaction Protocol (RTXP) inspired by Ryan Fugger's concepts shortly followed by the launch of the Ripple network.

- Just 10 months later XRP Fund II, LLC is established as a subsidiary of OpenCoin Inc. Bitcoin Bridge is introduced that enables users on the Ripple network to send payment to a Bitcoin wallet.
- In August 2013 XRP is made available to the public with airdrops and promotions.
- OpenCoin Inc. becomes Ripple Labs Inc in September 2013. Chris Larsen continues as the CEO. Ripple software became available as open source freeware.
- October 2013 – Ripple and ZipZap (US Money Transfer Company) enter into a partnership.
- Fidor Bank based in Munich, Germany becomes the first bank to start using Ripple in early 2014.
- In the last quarter of 2014 Cross River Bank and CBW Bank announce plans to use Ripple network. Also, Earthport, a global payments service provider, partners with Ripple.
- Ripple opens offices in Sydney, Australia in April 2015.
- London, UK, becomes the next Ripple international office in March 2016.

- ➢ In the summer of 2016 Ripple becomes only the fourth company with a BitLicense from New York State Department of Financial Services. In Japan a consortium of banks was formed to create a financial network using Ripple's underlying technology.
- ➢ Brad Garlinghouse takes over the reins of CEO in 2017 from Chris Larsen who continues as the Executive Chairman.
- ➢ An interbank group, Global Payments Steering Group, formed by Ripple to use the distributed network for international financial transactions and oversee the development of Ripple payment system, adds prominent members in spring of 2017 including Bank of America Merrill Lynch, Canadian Imperial Bank of Commerce and Standard Chartered.
- ➢ In 2018 Ripple announced it will release two new whitepapers; one that details XRP's Consensus Algorithm and the other that describes an algorithm to allow more validators.

How Does Ripple Work?

The fundamental concept of the Ripple network can be understood using the following example.

Let us say there are two persons, Rick and Sophie who live in towns that are miles apart. Rick wants to transfer $100 to Sophie. There are two financial agents, one in the same town as Rick and the other in the same location as Sophie. Let us name them Bob and Martin respectively. Bob and Martin know each other and act as intermediaries who transfer money among people. The above transaction will take place as follows.

> ➤ Rick will go to Bob and give him the money that he wants to send to Sophie. At the same time, Rick sends a password to Sophie. Rick also tells the password to Bob as well as the details of the transaction.
> ➤ Bob will contact Martin and provide him the details of the transaction as well as the password.
> ➤ Sophie will then go to Martin and provide him the password that Rick gave her.
> ➤ If Sophie's password matches the one that Martin received from Bob, Martin will pay Sophie $100.

In the above example, Bob did not pay Martin any money. Martin will instead create a record of the money owed to him by Bob in a ledger. Bob and

Martin come to an agreement called IOU (I Owe You) that states Bob owes Martin $100. Bob will agree to pay Martin at a later date or may make a similar transaction for Martin in the future.

The above example is a simplification of how the Ripple network operates, and Bob and Martin are likely to be institutions such as banks acting as 'Gateways'.

Gateways

In the Ripple network, gateways act as intermediaries and are used to send and receive supported currencies. Any individual or organization can operate a gateway. A transaction from a sender to a receiver might involve multiple gateways across different countries. Each gateway deals in a specific currency. The USDsnapswap is a gateway for US Dollars while the BTCbitstamp is a gateway for Bitcoins. There are multiple gateways on the Ripple network and a user can approach any one of these for transferring money.

Gateways may deal in Cryptocurrencies, fiat currencies and commodities like gold. Ripple allows interchange of the supported currencies and commodities. The sender can send US Dollars while the receiver can opt to receive Bitcoins. The sending and receiving gateways will maintain an IOU agreement that details the amount of money they might owe each other.

The system relies on trust between gateways. The gateways have to trust each other and build credibility over time. There may be cases where the sending and the receiving gateways do not directly trust each other. In such a scenario, there may be a common gateway that has good credibility with both of them and can act as an intermediary between the two for transfers.

In a case where there are no gateways to build a chain of trust between the sending and receiving gateways, then the transactions can be conducted using XRP.

Let us say that Rick has to transfer $100 to Sophie using gateways that do not trust each other.

Rick purchases XRP worth $100 at his gateway which then can transfer the XRP to the recipient gateway. The recipient gateway will then convert the XRP into the currency of Sophie's choosing and give the money to her. *As both gateways use XRP which is supported by the Ripple network across the globe, they can process transactions without worrying about inter-currency liabilities.* – This is a major innovation.

XRP Ledger (Ripple Consensus Protocol)

While Bitcoin and Ethereum use mining for processing transactions, Ripple makes use of the ledger consensus protocol now known as the XRP Ledger. The network consists of nodes which are computers that run Ripple server or client software. These nodes may be individually owned or run by financial institutions and banks that have partnered with Ripple. The network is decentralized as all the nodes are not under the control of a single entity.

The network uses a shared public ledger that contains immutable records of all the accounts and the transactions on the network. It also keeps track of all the IOUs between different gateways on the network. Server nodes across the globe update and maintain the ledger.

Before executing a transaction, the network has to verify that the transaction meets all the rules laid down by the network. A simple example of verification is to check if the transaction is a duplicate copy of another one. Transactions validators which are also known as validating nodes are used to verify the transactions.

Nodes on the network may receive different transactions. Each validating node selects some of the transactions after verification to add them to the ledger. The selected transactions are called candidate transactions.

All validating nodes on the network share their sets of candidate transactions with each other. The protocol then tries to determine a set that has been sent by most validating nodes. Once the majority of them agree on the same set of candidate transactions, the transactions of the set are processed and added to the ledger. The sharing and updating processes form a single round of consensus. The candidate transactions that were not processed may be taken up in the next round of consensus.

After every round of consensus, each validating node computes a new version of the ledger and compares it with other nodes. If a majority of the nodes have the same version of the ledger, it is then considered a validated ledger. Nodes whose ledger does not matches the validated ledger either re-compute their ledger or discard it and use the validated ledger obtained from other nodes.

Unique Node List

Ripple network verifies candidate transactions only if the majority of the nodes agree. Checking every node for verifying the transactions will be time-consuming. So, the network elects a few nodes that determine the transactions that must be processed and added to the ledger.

The group of these nodes is known as the Unique Node List (UNL). The nodes are selected based on their performance over time. When the majority of the nodes in the UNL list agree on a transaction, the shared public ledger is updated. As the verification process neither involves complex computation nor requires verification from multiple computers, it significantly increases the rate of transaction processing.

Users of the network can also choose UNL for processing transactions themselves. However, if the set of candidate transactions of the nodes in the UNL chosen by a user do not agree with those in the UNL recommended by Ripple, the transaction may not go through.

The XRP Ledger and UNL allow the Ripple network to process transactions faster than Bitcoin as well as traditional banking systems like SWIFT. The amount of fee charges is also significantly lower as the transactions involve fewer currency conversions.

Every transaction on the network costs a small amount of XRP. The XRP is destroyed instead of being distributed as transactions fees to prevent duplicate transactions and spams. XRP is not mined but was issued with a finite quantity of 100 Billion.

An XRP transaction can be processed in four seconds which is a lot less than a Bitcoin transaction that has been known to take up to an hour. The RippleNet can process 1500 transactions per second as compared to seven transactions per second of Bitcoin. Ripple has been continuously updating its infrastructure and technologies and has tested scaling capability of XRP to handle 50,000 transactions per second.

Ripple Controversies

The founders of Ripple retained 20% of the total created XRP for themselves at launch. The company owned the majority of the remaining XRP. The founders drew criticism for reserving a large amount of XRP. The controversy ended after the founders made it publicly know that they will sell their XRP slowly over the course of many years and won't dump it for short-term gains.

Ripple has time and again been the centre of discussions for not being truly decentralized. Also, the network uses fewer validation nodes for reaching consensus as compared to Bitcoin and Ethereum which is thought to make it more susceptible to attacks. The fact that the technical documentation of Ripple does not specify how the risks are mitigated further adds to the continuing speculation.

A few major cryptocurrency exchanges that did not have XRP on their websites were offered financial incentives by Ripple Labs for listing XRP. Even though the exchanges refused to list XRP, crypto enthusiasts and traders have frowned upon this legal, yet ethically questionable, approach by Ripple Labs.

How to Purchase and Trade XRP?

XRP is sold and traded at different cryptocurrency exchanges around the globe. Users can register on these exchanges and trade XRP and other currencies. The exchanges might require the users to undergo verification processes before they can start trading. The most popular cryptocurrency exchanges include:

- ➤ Binance
- ➤ Coinone
- ➤ OKEx
- ➤ Huobi
- ➤ Bitfinex
- ➤ Upbit
- ➤ Kraken
- ➤ Bitstamp
- ➤ Bittrex

XRP can be bought using fiat currencies, credit cards, and debit cards depending on the regulations of the country of purchase and the medium of purchase.

- ➤ **Bitcoins** – XRP can be purchased with Bitcoins from almost every cryptocurrency exchange.
- ➤ **Fiat Currencies** – Some currency exchanges allow users to purchase XRP with fiat currencies like Dollars, Pounds or Euros.
- ➤ **Altcoins** – XRP can be purchased using many altcoins.
- ➤ **Credit and Debit Cards** – XRP can be purchased using debit and credit cards. Some countries or exchanges might not allow credit cards for purchasing Cryptocurrencies.

It is important to get an XRP wallet before purchasing XRP. Just as a regular wallet is required to store printed fiat currencies, an XRP wallet is used to store XRP. Both software and hardware wallets are available for storing XRP.

Summarizing XRP

> ➢ Ripple is a global financial network consisting of banks, financial intuitions, and payment providers.
> ➢ XRP is a cryptocurrency or token used on the RippleNet.
> ➢ Ripple significantly improves the rate of processing currency transfer transactions while lowering the fees charged and electricity consumed.
> ➢ Ripple uses XRP Ledger (Ripple Consensus Protocol) instead of mining for verifying and processing transactions.
> ➢ The Ripple network supports exchange and transfer of fiat currencies like Dollars, Pounds or Euros, Cryptocurrencies and commodities.
> ➢ The network has gateways that can be banks or other financial institutions. These gate-

ways are used to send and receive currencies.

➢ Transactions are verified and processed by a
few selected validation nodes that form the
Unique Node List (UNL).

➢ XRP is the mode of payment on the Ripple
network for executing transactions. The XRP
charged is not distributed as transaction
fees but destroyed.

➢ Most prominent cryptocurrency exchanges
around the globe sell XRP.

XRP Quick Stats

Issue Date: 4 Aug 2013

Can be Mined: No

Issue Price: $0.005874

Peak Fiat Price to Date: $3.40 – 7 January 2018

Market Cap: $26,370,883,007 – 9 June 2018

Circulating Supply: 39,244,312,603 XRP

Available/Total Supply: 100 Billion XRP

Website: https://ripple.com

Chapter 15

Bitcoin Cash (BCH)

Bitcoin Cash is the fourth largest cryptocurrency by market capitalization making it the fourth most invested cryptocurrency in the world.

What is Bitcoin Cash?

Bitcoin Cash (Symbol: BCH) is a cryptocurrency used for financial transactions. It is a currency just like Dollars, Pounds or Euros but in digital format. It operates on a decentralized network and is not under the control of a single entity. Bitcoin Cash works on the same technology as Bitcoin and shares most of its fundamental concepts. It was created after a hard fork of the Bitcoin Blockchain.

What is a Cryptocurrency Fork?

A Blockchain verifies and processes transactions based on a set of rules or protocols. The rules or protocols of a Blockchain may be changed from time to time to improve the network, adding new features or reversing unfavorable situations like hacks or bugs. Any change in the rules of the Blockchain is called a *fork*. A fork upgrades the software of the Blockchain. However, some nodes on the network may run an older version of the software, while others may run the new version which may split the Blockchain into two different chains. One chain may consist of blocks with transactions from nodes running the old version of the software while the other chain may consist of blocks with transactions from nodes running the new version of the software.

This split might be temporary or permanent depending on the type of fork. There are two types of forks – soft forks and hard forks.

In a *soft fork*, the blocks of transactions processed by the nodes with the new version of the software are considered valid by the old version also. However, there may be instances wherein the blocks of transactions processed by the nodes with the old version of the software are not considered valid by the upgraded nodes. It is a temporary split which will be taken care of once all the nodes have upgraded their software to the new one.

A *hard fork* is a change in the rules that results in a permanent split in the Blockchain. The blocks of transactions processed by new nodes are considered invalid by old nodes and vice-versa. Each chain resulting from the split will maintain a separate ledger. The Blockchain that follows the older rules retains the token or cryptocurrency originally used while the new Blockchain will use a separate token.

A node that wants to process transactions according to the new rules will have to update its software. However, once it has done so, it will no longer be able to work as per old rules or add blocks of transactions to the older Blockchain.

Bitcoin Cash came into existence after a hard fork of the Bitcoin network. You could view it as a Bitcoin spinoff that follows a different set of protocols.

Why was Bitcoin Cash Needed?

Bitcoin Cash was needed as Bitcoin's block size was proving a significant limitation in the network. A block is a permanent record of a group of transactions on the network. It is like a page used to note down recent transactions. A transaction is only considered processed once it has been stored in a block. The Blockchain is composed of many such blocks in a linear order. Each block points to the block that comes immediately before it.

The Bitcoin network by design processes a new block once every ten minutes. Each block has a size limit of 1MB (megabyte). A 1MB block can record only a finite number of transactions. The actual number of transactions in a block may vary depending on the amount of information in each transaction. As the blocks have a pre-specified size limit and the Blockchain can add only one block every ten minutes, therefore only a few transactions can be processed within the stipulated time.

The time restriction on the creation of new blocks and the size limit of 1MB per block jointly constrained the transaction processing speed of the Bitcoin network which ranged upto 7 transactions per second. It came to be known as the Bitcoin scalability problem. The restrictions slowed the network, delayed the processing of transactions, and even increased the transaction fees.

As Bitcoin was a decentralized and opensource project overseen by a community comprising of individuals from around the globe, the members were free to voice their opinions. Some members of the community began to demand an increase in the block size of the Bitcoin Blockchain.

Roger Ver, an early Bitcoin investor and one of the founders of the Bitcoin Foundation, advocated for an increase in the block size. The increase would allow the Bitcoin network to process more transactions. Roger Ver devised a plan for implementing the same. Several other members of the Bitcoin community supported his endeavor. However, the community could not reach a consensus as some members wanted to double the block size while others wanted to increase it to 8MB. Eventually, proponents of the 8MB block size decided in favor of a hard fork and so Bitcoin Cash evolved.

History of Bitcoin Cash

- ➢ In 2016 Bitcoin's block size began limiting the processing capabilities of the network. The community set about finding a solution.
- ➢ Bitcoin ABC software was proposed to increase the block size to 8MB in June 2017. It was based on an algorithm from Bitmain, a company that produces hardware.
- ➢ "Bitcoin Cash" was the name recommended for the new cryptocurrency in July 2017 by

ViaBTC, a Chinese mining pool. The hard fork was set to be implemented at the block 478559 creating two different Blockchains.

➢ On 1 August 2017, the first block after the hard fork was created. Each Bitcoin holder received a pro-rata amount of Bitcoin Cash.

➢ November 2017 – Bitcoin changes its difficulty adjustment algorithm to improve stability.

➢ By 2018 Bitcoin Cash has rapidly become the fourth largest cryptocurrency by market capitalization.

How is Bitcoin Cash different from Bitcoin?

Bitcoin Cash implemented several protocols that separate its Blockchain from Bitcoin. The most significant change was the increase in the block size from 1MB to 8MB. The increase in the block size has made the Bitcoin Cash Blockchain faster than Bitcoin while reducing the fees charged for the transactions. Bitcoin has a scalable fee model. It processes transactions in blocks. Only one block is taken up for processing at a time. A block can contain only a finite number of transactions.

Imagine that each block can contain ten transactions and there are fifty transactions to be processed. A user on the Bitcoin network is free to choose the fee they are willing to pay for the transactions. Some users may pay a higher fee while others may pay a lower fee. The network will consider the ten transactions with the highest fee out of the fifty transactions. It will enlist these ten transactions to the block which will then become a part of the Blockchain.

The network will create a new block and will also receive new transactions. There are already forty pending transactions. If twenty new transactions were received, then a total of sixty transactions will compete for the ten slots in the new block. Out of these sixty, then ten transactions which are willing to pay the highest fees will be added. Users who want their transactions executed urgently will pay a higher fee. If the process continues, the processing fees will skyrocket and reach a point that might discourage users from using the network.

Bitcoin Cash overcame this limitation of Bitcoin by increasing the block size. It can process more transactions in each block while lowering the fees on the network.

Bitcoin Cash also implemented a new difficulty adjustment algorithm. While Bitcoin Cash originally used the Estimation of Distribution Algorithm (EDA), it caused heavy fluctuations in the processing capability of the network. In the EDA, the rate of creation of new blocks increased and decreased depending on the network demands. Miners found a way to bypass this by turning off their machines for several hours which lowered the processing power of the network and increased the blocks available. The miners then switched on their machines and processed a large number of transactions in a short time leading to quick profits.

The EDA algorithm was replaced by another one from the lead developer of Bitcoin Cash, Amaury Sechet. The new algorithm adjusts the rate of creation of blocks based on the network performance in the past twenty-four hours. The algorithm has a fixed limit of creating 144 blocks in a day which on average is equivalent to a block every ten minutes, like Ethereum. The number of blocks created in an hour may vary but the number of blocks created in twenty-four hours is 144. The new algorithm has made the network more stable and has been received positively by the community. With a more balanced creation of the blocks, the fees paid to the miners have also stabilised.

The Bitcoin Cash community is proposing another block size increase from 8MB to 32MB which will further improve the rate of processing transactions on the network while keeping fees lower. Bitcoin Cash developers are also working on introducing smart contracts into the Bitcoin Cash network. A smart contract is like a regular agreement but in digital form. It can be between two or more entities who want to conduct business with each other and use Bitcoin Cash as a payment medium. The agreement contains rules regarding the trade and the payable amount. The smart contract functionality will extend the capabilities of the Bitcoin Cash network and allow it to compete with Ethereum; although, to date, not enough is known to make any comparison

Controversies

Proponents of Bitcoin Cash consistently argue that it is closer to the vision that founder of Bitcoin Blockchain Santoshi Nakomoto had. They have repeatedly advocated that Bitcoin Cash is a true transactional currency and not a digital asset that Bitcoin appears to be evolving into.

AntPool, which is a major mining group began to burn (destroy) BCH coins. The primary purpose behind the move was to reduce the amount of BCH available which would create scarcity and increase its price. The move was seen as highly controversial by cryptocurrency communities.

Bitcoin Cash has a maximum supply of twenty-one million just like Bitcoin. A significant difference from Bitcoin is that miners will only be paid transaction fees once all the coins have been mined. This may be a possible disincentive to miners with short-term goals to monetize their investment.

How to Purchase and Trade Bitcoin Cash

Bitcoin Cash is sold and traded at different cryptocurrency exchanges around the globe. Users can register on these exchanges and trade Bitcoin Cash and other currencies. The exchanges might require the users to undergo verification processes before they can start trading. The most popular cryptocurrency exchanges include:

- ➢ Binance
- ➢ Coinbase
- ➢ OKEx
- ➢ Huobi
- ➢ Bitfinex
- ➢ Gdax
- ➢ Kraken
- ➢ Bitstamp
- ➢ Bittrex

Bitcoin Cash can be bought using fiat currencies, credit cards, and debit cards depending on the regulations of the country of purchase and the medium of purchase.

- ➤ **Bitcoins** – Bitcoin Cash can be purchased with Bitcoins from almost every cryptocurrency exchange.
- ➤ **Fiat Currencies** – Some currency exchanges allow users to purchase Bitcoin Cash with fiat currencies like Dollars, Pounds or Euros.
- ➤ **Altcoins** – Bitcoin Cash can be purchased using many altcoins.
- ➤ **Credit and Debit Cards** – Bitcoin Cash can be purchased using debit and credit cards. Some countries or exchanges might not allow credit cards for purchasing Cryptocurrencies.

It is important to get a Bitcoin Cash wallet before purchasing Bitcoin Cash. Just as a regular wallet is required to store printed fiat currencies, a Bitcoin Cash wallet is used to store Bitcoin Cash. Both software and hardware wallets are available for storing Bitcoin Cash.

Some wallets like BTC.com support both Bitcoin and Bitcoin Cash. A user must ensure that they do not accidentally send Bitcoins to a Bitcoin Cash account or vice versa as it may lead to the loss of funds.

Summarizing Bitcoin Cash

- ➤ Bitcoin Cash's principal purpose is as a currency.
- ➤ Bitcoin Cash is a branch-off from the Bitcoin that follows a different set of rules. It emerged after a hard fork of the Bitcoin Blockchain.
- ➤ Bitcoin Cash was envisioned to tackle the Bitcoin block size limitation that restricted the transaction processing rate and led to higher the fees.
- ➤ It was launched on 1 August 2017 and block 478559 was the first to be processed. Every owner of Bitcoin received a pro-rata equivalent amount of Bitcoin Cash.
- ➤ Bitcoin Cash increased the block size limit from 1MB to 8MB increasing the transactions processing rate while lowering fees.
- ➤ Bitcoin Cash uses a difficulty adjustment algorithm that adjusts the rate of creation of new blocks on an hourly basis but produces a fixed 144 blocks in a day.

- ➢ The Bitcoin Cash community is working on further improvements to the network speed while lowering fees.

Bitcoin Cash Quick Stats

Issue Date: 1 August 2017

Can be Mined: Yes

Issue Price: $555.89

Peak Fiat Price to Date: $3,785.82 – 20 December 2017

Market Cap: $16,269,032,115 –

Circulating Supply: 17,178,750 BCH – 12 June 2018

Available/Total Supply: 21,000,000 BCH

Website: https://www.Bitcoincash.org

Chapter 16

EOS

EOS is the fifth largest cryptocurrency by market capitalisation, making it the fifth most invested cryptocurrency in the world. It's ascendancy to a Top 5 Crypto is remarkable, achieved in less than a year.

What are EOSIO and EOS?

EOSIO is an open-source software based on the Blockchain technology. It uses an architecture much like an operating system, that allows developers to build Decentralised Applications (DApps) to run on the EOSIO Blockchain. The network can be scaled vertically and horizontally which enables it to process up to 300,000 transactions per second with a stated aim to increase to 1 million. It also eliminates fees for the end-users.

EOS is a token or a cryptocurrency that is used on the EOSIO Blockchain network. It is used to pay for the resources and services on the Blockchain. The amount of EOS held by an individual or an organisation will determine the bandwidth and storage space available to the holder on the EOSIO network. If a person owns 3% of total EOS tokens, they can use up to 3% of the network's bandwidth or storage.

Why is EOSIO needed?

Blockchain technology attracted attention after the launch of the Bitcoin cryptocurrency. While Bitcoin used Blockchain for currency transfer, developers of different Blockchain platforms have tried to employ the technology for building applications that run on their decentralized networks, most notably Ethereum. They have faced many challenges while doing the same. The developers have struggled to increase the computational capacity of the network for efficiently processing thousands of transactions per second. Another issue has been the high fees charged from the users of the network. EOSIO is a decentralised network based on the Blockchain technology that aims to provide excellent processing capability for running decentralised applications while keeping fees low or eliminating them altogether. EOSIO is striving to ensure widespread adoption of the Blockchain technology across different spheres and can be considered a direct competitor to Etheruem.

History

- ➢ EOSIO is introduced in May 2017 by block.one who oversee the project. Daniel Larimer is the CTO of block.one.
- ➢ EOS code is made publicly available for review on 1 June 2017.
- ➢ Distribution of EOS token commenced on 26 June and EOS started trading on exchanges on 1 July 2017.
- ➢ EOSIO Single-Threaded Application Test net (STAT), a testing environment, made available to the public in November 2017.
- ➢ On 31 January 2018 the Alpha version of the platform is released.
- ➢ 10 June 2018 – EOSIO 'main net' Blockchain is launched.

EOSIO Blockchain

As EOSIO is based on Blockchain technology, it verifies transactions in blocks. A block can contain a finite number of transactions. A transaction is only processed once it has been added to a block. Once a block has been processed, it is appended to the shared public ledger which stores immutable records of accounts and transactions on the network.

The blocks are produced by nodes on the network. A node is a computer that is running the EOS software. A node can also act as a validating node or an API (Application Programming Interface) service node for Chain or Wallet, or it can perform all three functions simultaneously. Validating nodes are responsible for verifying and processing transactions. An API service node is used by developers to code applications that use the EOSIO Blockchain.

The EOS.IO network makes use of a decentralized consensus algorithm known as Delegated Proof of Stake (DPoS). The DPoS algorithm performs two primary functions.

First of all, it selects block producers. The producers are elected in such a way so that the stakeholders have complete control of the network for ensuring its smooth operation. A stakeholder is someone who owns EOS. Each stakeholder in the network is allowed to vote for selecting block producers. The process is called approval voting. The weight of their vote will depend on the amount of stake they hold.

The number of block producers selected is decided by the stakeholders. The number is chosen in such a way so that at least 50% of voting stakeholders believe that the network has sufficient decentralization. If there are ten stakeholders, and five of them believe that there should be at least thirty block producers to ensure decentralization of the network, then there are thirty block producers created. The block producers are paid for creating new blocks. The list of active block producers is updated once every day. The network must have at least twenty-one block producers.

Once the block producers have been selected, the next step involves scheduling the production of blocks. The Blockchain that the twenty-one nodes agree on will be copied by all the nodes on the network.

What makes EOS different?

It's Delegated Proof of Stake consensus is unique and fundamentally different from Proof of Stake with the major benefit being the speed of transaction processing and validating.

The EOSIO Blockchain intends to make the network free for the end-user. Consider a website like Amazon where a user does not pay for visiting the website. All hosting and maintenance costs of the website are borne by the Amazon company itself. The company makes profits by charging a commission on the products sold from its website. EOSIO is aiming to create a Blockchain platform based on the same principle. The platform will be free for the end user, but the senders or the application developers utilising the platform will have to pay for it.

The EOSIO platform supports the development of software applications that utilise the Blockchain. It will also have smart contract functionality. A smart contract is similar to current real-world contracts. A contract is an agreement that might specify financial transactions, legally binding relationships between entities or other actionable information whose outcome is governed by rules. An EOSIO smart contract is similarly a digital agreement stored on the Blockchain. It can be used to trade currency, shares, commodities or anything else that might have value just like real-world contracts which are written and enforcable in law.

EOSIO network has low latency, which means faster transactions and fewer delays. It also has fast sequential processing capability that allows it to support high-performance applications such as exchanges. All the accounts on the network have human-readable names up to 12 characters long that can be chosen by the account users themselves.

EOSIO Controversies

EOSIO received criticism in early stages of development due to the lack of availability of a whitepaper that described the technical aspects of the project in detail. The whitepaper was released at a later date.

Block.one was also criticised for not having a working model while running a campaign to raise money for funding their project. Nevertheless, its meteoric rise to a Top 5 Cryptocurrency in less than a year is testament to its potential wide-ranging global utility.

How to Purchase and Trade EOS

EOS can be traded at different cryptocurrency exchanges around the globe. Users can register on these exchanges and trade EOS and other currencies. The exchanges might require the users to undergo verification processes before they can start trading. The most popular cryptocurrency exchanges include:

- ➤ Binance
- ➤ Coinex
- ➤ OKEx
- ➤ Huobi
- ➤ Bitfinex
- ➤ Upbit
- ➤ Kraken
- ➤ Gate.io
- ➤ HitBTC

- ➤ **Bitcoins** – EOS can be exchanged with Bitcoins from almost every cryptocurrency exchange.
- ➤ **Altcoins** – EOS can be exchanged using some altcoins.

It is important to get an EOS wallet before purchasing EOS. Both software and hardware wallets are available for storing EOS.

Summarizing EOSIO

- ➢ EOSIO is an open-source platform based on Blockchain that is designed to support a wide array of applications.
- ➢ EOS is the token or cryptocurrency that is used to pay for the network's resources.
- ➢ It aims to provide a Blockchain network that can process thousands of transactions while making it free for the end-user.
- ➢ EOSIO makes use of the Delegated Proof of Stake (DPoS) consensus algorithm.
- ➢ The network consists of at least twenty-one block producing nodes that are selected by votes of the stakeholders.
- ➢ EOSIO supports smart contract which are like legally binding agreements.
- ➢ The network has fewer delays, supports sequential processing and has human-readable account names.
- ➢ EOSIO went 'live' in June 2018 and so is still early stage and its real-world application is yet to be proven.

X Quick Stats

Issue Date: 26 June 2017 (ICO)

Can be Mined: No

Issue Price: $0.99 (ICO Token Price)

Peak Fiat Price to Date: $22.71 – 29 April 2018

Market Cap: $8,728,065,902 – 13 June 2018

Circulating Supply: 896,149,492 EOS

Total Supply: 1 Billion

Website: https://eos.io

Chapter 17

Litecoin (LTC)

Litecoin is the sixth largest cryptocurrency by market capitalization after Bitcoin making it the sixth most invested cryptocurrency in the world.

What is Litecoin?

Litecoin is a cryptocurrency based on a decentralized payment network that draws inspiration from the Bitcoin Blockchain. It is an open source project that is not under the control of a central entity. Litecoins are transferred on the Internet and may be used to pay for different goods and services from companies who accept it as a form of payment. It is characterised by its low fees and fast transaction processing.

Why was Litecoin created?

Litecoin was created from the code of the Bitcoin Core client. The Bitcoin Core client is the software responsible for running and maintaining the Bitcoin Blockchain. It changed a few rules or protocols of the software that resulted in a different Blockchain and cryptocurrency. The main changes made included:

> ➢ Reduction in block creation time from 10 minutes to 2.5 minutes.
> ➢ A memory-hard scrypt based proof-of-work algorithm for mining.
> ➢ Increase in the supply limit of Litecoins to 84 million which is four times Bitcoins (21 million).

A Blockchain network processes transactions in groups known as blocks. The Litecoin network was created to reduce the block creation time from Bitcoin's one block every 10 minutes to Litecoin's one block every 2.5 minutes. The slow block processing rate of Bitcoin had choked the network and had increased the time required for processing transactions. It had also resulted in high transaction fees on the network. By lowering the block creation time, the Litecoin network was able to process more transactions while lowering the fees.

The Blockchain technology uses a process called mining for verifying and processing transactions. The

Bitcoin Blockchain uses the SHA-256 algorithm which is not memory-hard. It allowed devices such as ASIC and FPGA miners to mine Bitcoins at a faster rate than regular CPUs and GPUs. These devices were expensive and out of reach of most people. There was a probability that it would allow ASIC miners to control the network as they would hold the majority of the processing capability of the network. They would be able to have a greater influence on the decisions regarding changes in the network. It would defeat the primary purpose of making Bitcoin a decentralized network. Litecoin overcame the same by implementing scrypt functionality in its Proof-of-Work (PoW) mining algorithm making it memory-hard. It made the creation of the ASIC miners for Litecoins harder and more expensive. At the same time, it also allowed people with regular computers to mine Litecoin using their CPUs and GPUs.

History of Litecoin

- ➤ Charlie Lee starts development on the Lite-coin using the code from the bitcoin client and a proof-of-work algorithm with scrypt function.

- ➢ On 7 October 2011, Charlie Lee makes the open source client for Litecoin publicly available on Github.
- ➢ The Litecoin network went online six days later on 13 October 2011.
- ➢ In November 2013 Litecoin crossed $1 billion market capitalization. Various vulnerabilities on the network are fixed to improve security.
- ➢ A new version of Litecoin is released in December 2013, lowering the transaction fees.
- ➢ Litecoin implements the Lightning Network protocol via SegWit upgrade in May 2017 for conducting microtransactions instantly.
- ➢ Alza, an e-commerce website based in the Czech Republic, started accepting Litecoin in February 2018 rapidly followed by many others.

Litecoin Blockchain

Litecoin works on Blockchain technology just like Bitcoin. The network consists of nodes which are computers running the Litecoin software. Each node is responsible for verifying and processing transactions. The transactions are processed in blocks which are created every 2.5 minutes. A block can contain a finite number of transactions. The nodes process transactions by performing complex mathematical calculations and add them to a block. The nodes compete with each other for getting their block added first. The node whose block is the first to be added to the network is rewarded with Litecoins.

Litecoin, like Bitcoin, makes use of a Proof-of-Work (PoW) mining algorithm. However, the Litecoin Blockchain uses an algorithm with the scrypt hash function instead of the SHA-256 used by the Bitcoin Blockchain. A hash function is a complex mathematical calculation performed to verify and process a transaction and add it to the Blockchain.

The hash function adjusts the difficulty of the network every 2,016 blocks which is approximately 3.5 days. It increases or decreases the difficulty depending on the total time taken for mining the previous 2,016 blocks. The objective of increasing or decreasing the difficulty is to maintain a consistent block generation rate of 2.5 minutes or 2,016 blocks every 3.5 days. If the creation of the previous 2,016 blocks took more than 3.5 days, the difficulty reduces. If they were created in less than 3.5 days, the difficulty increases.

The amount of Litecoin rewarded to miners halves every 840,000 blocks. Considering its block creation time of 2.5 minutes, halving happens once every four years. The reward was first reduced from 50LTC to 25LTC on 25 August 2015. The next reduction will happen in August 2019 which will halve the reward from 25LTC to 12.5LTC.

Individuals who want to mine Litecoin, install its software on their computers. The software runs the algorithm and performs the mathematical calculations required using the hash function. Each calculation may have multiple valid solutions. Every time miners solve the function successfully, they create a block that is added to the Blockchain and are rewarded with Litecoins.

The computers have to check every possible solution to the problem before they can arrive at the correct one. The computers must have high computational power (hash rate) to be able to solve the hash function. While both algorithms are computationally intensive, the scrypt is also memory intensive. It means that the amount of RAM (Random Access Memory) required for scrypt based algorithms is a lot more than SHA-256 based algorithms.

It narrows down the difference between the hash rate of CPUs and GPUs as compared to ASIC miners.

An ASIC miner is special hardware designed for mining cryptocurrencies. It has higher computational power than CPUs and GPUs. Computer miners can't compete with ASIC miners which puts them at a disadvantage. Scrypt algorithms were designed to minimize the difference between ASIC miners and computer miners and put them on a level position. It would allow everyone an equal opportunity to be a part of the Litecoin platform. However, with time, ASIC miners have been developed that can mine Litecoin.

At the time of writing, more than 57,000,000 LTC have been mined which is more than 66% of the total 84,000,000. However, as the reward for mining Litecoins decreases every four years, the number of newly mined Litecoins also decreases. Theoretically, if the block creation time of Litecoin stays at 2.5 seconds and the reward keeps on halving every four years, it might take up to the year 2143 to mine all Litecoins.

Litecoin Controversies

Charlie Lee sold/donated all of his Litecoins which created a controversy in the community. He defended himself stating it was a conflict of interest for him to own a cryptocurrency whose development he was overseeing. He confirmed that he was intent on continuing devoting his time to the development of Litecoin.

Litecoin underwent a hard fork in February of 2018 that led to the creation of the Litecoin Cash (LCC) cryptocurrency platform. The new platform uses the LCC tokens, and every holder of the Litecoin with a wallet received ten LCC tokens for each LTC token they had. Litecoin Cash aims to improve the transaction processing speed and uses the SHA256 mining technique like Bitcoin. The creation was discouraged by Litecoin's founder Charlie Lee as well as the majority of Litecoin community. Charlie Lee himself tweeted:

"The Litecoin team and I are not forking Litecoin. Any fork that you hear about is a scam trying to confuse you to think it's related to Litecoin. Don't fall for it and definitely don't enter your private keys or seed into their website or client. Be careful out there!"

Litecoin Cash (LCC) did not attract enough attention even though the fork was successful.

How to Purchase and Trade Litecoin

Litecoin is sold and traded at different cryptocurrency exchanges around the globe. Users can register on these exchanges and trade Litecoin and other currencies. The exchanges might require the users to undergo verification processes before they can start trading. The most popular cryptocurrency exchanges include:

- ➢ Binance
- ➢ GDAX
- ➢ BTC China
- ➢ Huobi
- ➢ Bitfinex
- ➢ WEX
- ➢ Kraken
- ➢ OKCoin
- ➢ Bittrex

Litecoins can be bought using fiat currencies, credit cards, and debit cards depending on the regulations of the country of purchase and the medium of purchase.

- ➢ **Bitcoins** – Litecoins can be purchased with Bitcoins from almost every cryptocurrency exchange.
- ➢ **Fiat Currencies** – Some currency exchanges allow users to purchase Litecoin with fiat currencies like Dollars, Pounds or Euros.
- ➢ **Altcoins** – Litecoin can be purchased using many altcoins.

> ➤ **Credit and Debit Cards** – Litecoins can be purchased using debit and credit cards. Some countries or exchanges might not allow credit cards for purchasing cryptocurrencies.

It is important to get a Litecoin wallet before purchasing Litecoins. Just as a regular wallet is required to store printed fiat currencies, a Litecoin wallet is used to store Litecoin. Both software and hardware wallets are available for storing Litecoins.

Summarizing Litecoin

> ➤ Litecoin is the sixth largest cryptocurrency by market capitalization.
> ➤ It is based on the Bitcoin Core client and was created by Charlie Lee in October 2011.
> ➤ Litecoin aimed to reduce the block creation time to 2.5 minutes as compared to the 10 minutes taken by the Bitcoin Blockchain.
> ➤ Litecoin uses a scrypt based Proof-of-Work (PoW) algorithm for mining to make it ASIC-resistant.
> ➤ The total amount of Litecoins available is 84 million.

Litecoin Quick Stats

Issue Date: 13 July 2012

Can be Mined: Yes

Issue Price: $0.0325

Peak Fiat Price to Date: $360.66 – 18 December 2017

Market Cap: $5,547,075,714 – 15 June 2018

Circulating Supply: 56,989,821 LTC – 15 June 2018

Total Supply: 84,000,000 LTC

Website: https://litecoin.org

POSTSCRIPT

You may recall from Chapter 1 that back in 2013 when I first chanced upon Bitcoin and cryptocurrencies I spent three weeks researching the subject. As a result of that in-depth research I decided to mine a cryptocurrency called Quark. I corralled all of my family's computers into working 24 hours a day mining the Quark with a real sense of anticipation that this was *'the one'*. It didn't take long before I had to reduce down to my sole laptop after protests from my family about their computers slowing right down as a result of my mining activities. I confess that I haven't ever checked the effect on our electricity consumption at the time.

To update you on the current state of play. I'm pleased to inform you that Quark has stayed the course, just! In 2014 it peaked at a little over $0.24; this was its nadir and in retrospect I wonder if the result of a Pump and Dump. The price, today as I write, $0.0008. Yes, it's lost 99.96% of its value!

At least I bought some Bitcoin.

GLOSSARY

Airdrop	Free give-away of cryptocurrency, usually to current holders.
Altcoins	A generic term for all other Cryptocurrencies other than Bitcoin.
ASIC	Application-Specific Integrated Circuit – powerful computers configured to mine a specified cryptocurrency only. No MS Office or YouTube here!
Atomic Swaps	Allowing 2 persons on different Blockchains to directly exchange tokens without need for an inter-mediary
Blockchain	Software which provides an immutable record of transactions conducted on it
BTC	Bitcoin - Used to designate a Bitcoin
Cold wallet	A cryptocurrency wallet not held on any electronic device such as PC

	or on the Internet
Crypto	Shortened version of cryptocurrency
DApp	Decentralised Application
DL	Distributed Ledger - a ledger distributed across the blockchain
DLT	Distributed Ledger Technology
Double Spend	If someone tries to spend their Bitcoins to two different recipients at the same time, this is double spending. Bitcoin protocols on the Blockchain prevent this; only one transaction will be allowed through thus preventing fraud.
DPoS	Delegated Proof of Stake
ETH	Ether, the token used on the Ethereum block chain
Fiat currency	A paper currency issued by a national government/central bank. For example, US dollars, British pounds, European euros, etc.
FOMO	Fear of Missing Out

GFC	Global Financial Crisis
Hard Fork	Fundamental change in the Blockchain software of a crypto currency not agreed by consensus and so resulting in a new version of the cryptocurrency. Example being Bitcoin Cash from Bitcoin.
Hodl	Hold - crypto enthusiasts term for continuing to hold a particular cryptocurrency
Hot wallet	A cryptocurrency wallet that requires an Internet connection to be opened
Lightning	A protocol being developed to significantly increase transaction rate for Bitcoin and Litecoin.
Mining	Using a computer to solve complex mathematical calculations for the Bitcoin network to confirm transactions. Miners who successfully solve calculations are rewarded with Bitcoin as well as receiving transaction fees for the transactions they confirm.

Ponzi	A Ponzi is a fraudulent investment operation that pays returns to its investors from their own money, or the money paid by subsequent investors. Eventually there are no new investors, or not enough of them, and the scheme collapses.
PoS	Proof of Stake
PoW	Proof of Work
Pyramid Scheme	See Ponzi above
SegWit	Segregated Witness
Soft Fork	Change in the cryptocurrency Blockchain software agreed by consensus so effectively upgrades the cryptocurrency.
Trustless	Powerful security enabled by there being no intermediary within the Blockchain transaction.
White Paper	Document detailing the Vision, Purpose, Plan for, and Execution of, a Blockchain and its associated cryptocurrency.

End Note

For those interested in developing their knowledge further the author, Martin May-Clingo, is offering training seminars in Europe and Southeast Asia. You can follow him on the popular social media channels and website as follows:

www.Bitcoin-4-Beginners.com

Facebook - Bitcoin4BeginnersWorld

Twitter - @4Beginners

LinkedIn - Martin May-Clingo

CPSIA information can be obtained
at www.ICGtesting.com
Printed in the USA
LVHW081726250221
679917LV00043B/1605